kiddiwalks in

Lincolnshire

D0263830

Catherine W. Smith

COUNTRYSIDE BOOKS
NEWBURY BERKSHIRE

05020045

COUNTRYSIDE BOOKS
3 Catherine Road
Newbury, Berkshire

To view our complete range of books,
please visit us at
www.countrysidebooks.co.uk

ISBN 978 1 84674 284 2

Designed by Peter Davies, Nautilus Design
Produced through MRM Associates Ltd., Reading
Typeset by Jean Cussons Typesetting, Diss, Norfolk
Printed by Information Press, Oxford

Contents

AREA MAP SHOWING LOCATION OF THE WALKS

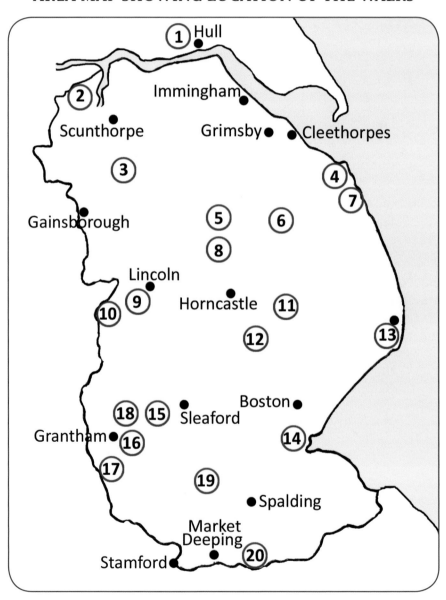

Contents

PUBLISHER'S NOTE

We hope that you obtain considerable enjoyment from this book; great care has been taken in its preparation. Although at the time of publication all routes followed public rights of way or permitted paths, diversion orders can be made and permissions withdrawn.

We cannot, of course, be held responsible for such diversion orders and any inaccuracies in the text which result from these or any other changes to the routes, nor any damage which might result from walkers trespassing on private property. We are anxious though that all details covering the walks are kept up to date and would therefore welcome information from readers which would be relevant to future editions.

The simple sketch maps that accompany the walks in this book are based on notes made by the author whilst checking out the routes on the ground. They are designed to show you how to reach the start, to point out the main features of the overall circuit and they contain a progression of numbers that relate to the paragraphs of the text.

However, for the benefit of a proper map, we do recommend that you purchase the relevant Ordnance Survey sheet covering your walk. The Ordnance Survey maps are widely available, especially through booksellers and local newsagents.

Introduction

Lincolnshire is very special. Lincolnshire sits there – quietly, modestly – serving agriculture, air force bases and the north-south fast train links. Yet, as one of England's largest counties, it has become one of the most diverse and extraordinary areas in England.

Lincolnshire does not offer just one type of walk. It can offer much more! It is divided into several areas, the vales, the fens, the Wash, the wolds and the north. Each area of beauty brings with it a diverse landscape. The lush green vales to the south-west provide wonderful canal walks and beautiful hilly countryside. The fens to the south-east offer the chance to see the wetlands supporting wildlife and habitats. The Wash brings us wonderful coastal walks any time of the year. The wonder of the wolds in the middle of Lincolnshire is rich with stunning woodland and quaint towns. The north brings us close to the moors and peatland, and around the whole of the county are farms of every type.

Deeping Lakes, featured in Walk 20.

Then there is Lincolnshire's famous aviation history which is evident throughout, from the Red Arrows at RAF Scampton outside Lincoln, to the history of the Dambusters at Woodhall Spa, and today's east-coast bombing range near Mablethorpe.

This wonderful combination helps make walking fun for children who need variety to hold their interest. The walks I have chosen do just that. They range from coastal, to canal, farmland, countryside, woodland and forest. I strongly encourage you to try different routes to offer your child a real insight into the seasonal, habitat and geographical variety around them.

I have included a section called 'Making the Most of Your Day', which lists free or cheap activities nearby which will appeal to families. I hope I can encourage you to travel further afield in Lincolnshire to explore the county and use one of these extra suggestions to round off a day out without great expense. It really is worth it.

These 'adventures' come with suggestions for games and fun things to do on the way. Your children can make up their own games as they go along, or they might like to use some of the ideas here. Picnics are great for making a walk 'an adventure' and I've indicated where good picnic places can be found, including my own 'favourite picnic stops'.

Walking the great outdoors is meant to be fun for the whole family. I sincerely hope that you will all, like my family, enjoy the freedom and adventure Lincolnshire has to offer. Remember – it's not a walk, it's an adventure …

Catherine W. Smith

Acknowledgements

A big 'well done' to Darcey and Kaelin who accompanied me on these walks and didn't complain once. Your opinions were very helpful! Thank you also to Ian whose steady artistic skills in drawing the maps were greatly appreciated. Finally, thank you to John Pinchbeck for his local and historical knowledge and for casting a second pair of eyes over my work.

1

Humber Bridge Country Park

The Cliff Trail

Lush woodland paths.

The Humber Bridge is a mighty statement in North Lincolnshire and makes for an impressive climb high above the estuary to reach the Humber Bridge Country Park. The park offers weaving trails and lots of climbing up the side of banks – every young explorer's delight! At the end of all this fun, you can enjoy the play area overlooking the Humber Bridge.

Getting there *From the A15 Barton-upon-Humber road, head towards the toll on Humber Bridge. Check toll bridge charges at www.humberbridge. co.uk/toll. Once you have crossed the bridge, stay left at the toll booth. The country park is well signposted immediately on your left from here.*

Length of walk 2 miles.
Time Allow 2 hours.
Terrain A mixture of flat and hilly areas. Suitable for pushchairs and bikes.
Dogs No restrictions. Keep dogs under control.
Start/Parking Free parking at Humber Bridge Country Park. Drive through the first car park into the second one by the Tourist Information Centre. (GR TA022258).

Map OS Explorer 293 Kingston upon Hull and Beverley.
Refreshments Mrs B's Woodland Café in the country park, serving hot and cold food, snacks and refreshments. Picnic tables are widely available. There are toilets in the car park and at the play area.

1 The Cliff Trail usually begins at the Black Mill on the Hessle foreshore, but if you are not local, it is easier to start from the country park car park. This trail is not marked on the way round, so it is advisable to use a map. From Mrs B's Woodland Café, you will see a footpath leading into the park. Go into the park and turn left, following the signs which take you right, towards a metal gate with steps leading down into the park. (If you have a country park map from the tourist

◆ Fun Things to See and Do ◆

Climbing. The steep banks of the former chalk quarry are ideal for children to try a spot of mountaineering. There are also places in the woods where they can practise their climbing skills, as well as exploring the many tracks that trail off the main paths.

Kiddiwalks in Lincolnshire

The Walk

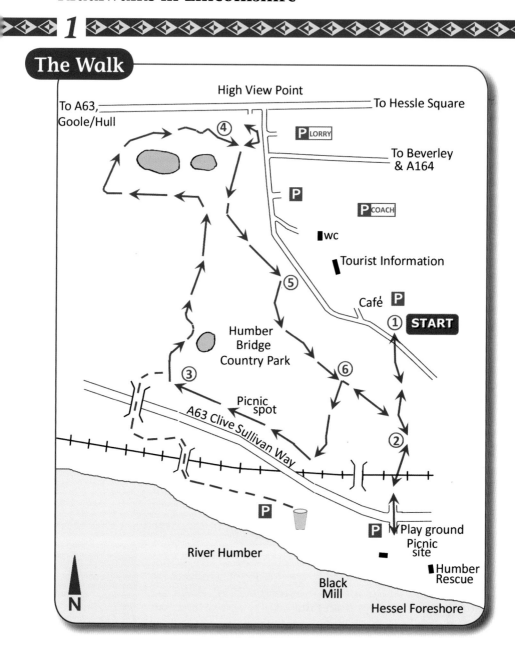

High View Point

To A63, Goole/Hull

To Hessle Square

P LORRY

④

To Beverley & A164

P

P COACH

WC

Tourist Information

Café P

① START

⑤

Humber Bridge Country Park

③

⑥

Picnic spot

A63 Clive Sullivan Way

②

P

River Humber

P Play ground
Picnic site

Humber Rescue

Black Mill

N

Hessel Foreshore

information office, this first section is marked in yellow to the Little Switzerland entrance.) Once at the bottom of the steps you will see a quarry bank to your left, and a bench. Children love climbing up this bank, though getting back down is considerably harder!

2 From the bench turn right and follow the path. You will approach a small meadow to your left which makes a popular picnic spot. Continue, then take the first left turn and follow the path round. On this pathway, there is a large green area on your left which is ideal for ball games. This pretty place is my favourite **picnic stop**. From the picnic bench you can often see groups of climbers on top of the Humber Bridge.

3 Continue left along the edge of the park until you reach a road. Just before the end of the road there is a right turn into the woodland. Follow this path which offers lots of climbing on the side of the banks and hidden trails. Try to spot the tree with giant roots! Continue along this path until you reach a bench beside an owl sculpture. Bear left and continue to climb as you follow the trail round. You will

eventually see a large pond on your right. If you wish to explore the ponds, there are steps further along leading down. Dogs are very keen on the ponds and you may see quite a few swimming and playing. Bear this in mind if you have children who are not keen on dogs. Once you have finished exploring the ponds, take the steps back up to rejoin the Cliff Trail.

4 As you continue to curve around the trail you will see the High View Point and steep steps. We visited this viewpoint, but all we could see were a few tree tops, so if you have a pushchair, bike or young children you might want to give this a miss without feeling guilty. Continue past the steps and follow the trail until you approach a wooden bridge. Cross the bridge and bear left. When you reach another fork in the path, bear left again.

5 Continue along to the wooden steps. Climb these and continue ahead by the wooden phoenix sculptures.

6 Follow the trail as it merges with the path you followed on the way in and leads you back to the bench by the quarry and steps. If you want to explore the estuary

11 ◆

and play area, turn right and follow the path over two footbridges. This leads you to Hessle foreshore where you can stand on the bank of the estuary and have a magnificent view of the Humber Bridge. Otherwise, climb the steps back to the café and car park.

The mighty Humber Bridge.

◆ Background Notes ◆

The Humber Bridge connects North Lincolnshire with Yorkshire and was opened by The Queen in 1981, having taken nine years to build. It is a mass of steel and concrete which has saved motorists many miles, and brought these two counties closer together. The Humber Bridge Country Park was a chalk quarry until 1960 and has since been developed into an area of natural beauty. Crossing this bridge is part of the experience and will be enjoyed by the children.

MAKING THE MOST OF YOUR DAY

- **Hessle foreshore.** Walk along this bank for views of the bridge and estuary. There is also a play area, a disused windmill called Black Mill, toilets and the Country Park Inn which has a full bar and restaurant.
- **Thornton Abbey, and the Abbots Garden**, near Ulceby, south of the river. Something different for the summer. Find your way through the Maize Maze, picnic in the abbey grounds, do some fruit picking and much more. www.abbotsgarden.co.uk
- **The Deep** – the famous aquarium in central Hull, with sharks and the world's first submarium. www.thedeep.co.uk

Crowle Moor

The Decoy Trail

Black Hebridean sheep live on the reserve.

This walk in the north-west of Lincolnshire really does make you feel as though you have stepped into the next county. We are now on the moors of the Humberhead Peatlands, an area of bog wilderness and conservation. This adventure explores the bog-life of the moors and, in doing so, is unlike any of the other walks in this book. There are also beautiful views across the moors.

Kiddiwalks in Lincolnshire

2

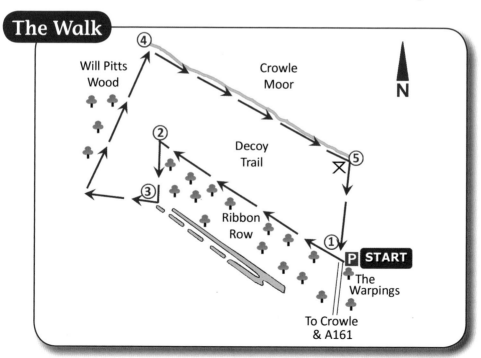

Getting there *From the A161, head north-west through Crowle village. Follow the brown National Nature Reserve signs (a white duck on a brown background) through the village until you reach a single-track road across farmland. At the end of the road turn right (by the NNR sign). Be aware that from this point the road is unclassified and very uneven. Less than half a mile from here you will see a 'Natural England' noticeboard on your left, where you can park.*

Length of walk 2¾ miles.
Time Allow 2 hours.
Terrain Flat, but very uneven in places so not suitable for pushchairs. It can also be boggy and muddy underfoot in winter so wellies are recommended.
Dogs Dogs must be on a lead in the conservation area.
Start/Parking Free parking at Crowle Moor (GR SE759145).
Map OS Explorer 280 Isle of Axholme.
Refreshments The nearest café is on the main road through Crowle. There are limited places

The Walk

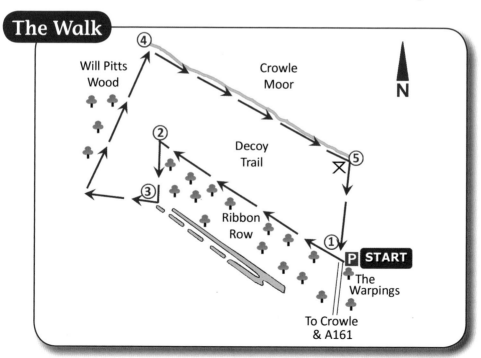

Will Pitts Wood
Crowle Moor
N
④
②
Decoy Trail
③
⑤
Ribbon Row
①
P START
The Warpings
To Crowle & A161

to stop for a rest on this walk but my favourite picnic stop is at point 4. Take a small rug to sit on and keep an eye on small children near the water's edge.

1 From the car park, climb over the wooden gate into the nature reserve. Continue until you reach another gate. Go through this and continue ahead. Look out on your right for black Hebridean sheep flocking together. On your left are bog areas. There are also lots of ferns and heather.

2 Climb a third wooden gate, where the path curves round to the left by a waymarker post. On

this section, more bogs appear either side of your path.

3 After following this stretch you come to a waymarker leading to your right. If at this point you wish to extend your walk to the Viewing Tower, go left (it will add approximately 2 miles to your walk). Otherwise, follow the path right. On your left you will see Will Pitts Wood. After walking through an enclosure of trees, you pass a further waymarker and turn right. This section runs parallel with a river/ditch. I found this section can be a bit long for small children as the path is narrow and the vegetation grows

◆ Fun Things to See and Do ◆

Nature Walk. Take binoculars and a magnifying glass. Look out for Hebridean sheep, purple heather, bog insects, heath butterflies and nightingales. There are also different types of grasses growing beside the bogs including bog rosemary, common cotton grass and cranberry. Encourage the children to look closely at these things and use their magnifying glass. www.wildlifewatch.org.uk has various nature spotting sheets that you can print off.

Mud dollies. If you can cope with this one in the damp weather when it is muddy underfoot, grab some handfuls of mud and mould it in your hands to make a mud dolly (you could use disposable gloves). Make use of natural things on the ground, such as fern, leaves or stones to create the outfit and hair. Children love mud and it washes off easily.

high, leaving them with little to see. To keep them interested why not have a nature quiz as you walk? Try www.outdoor-nature-child.com for inspirational questions.

4 Continue down this path until you come to a waymarker. Turn right down a small embankment and continue ahead. The interest picks up again as you pass a very large bog on the right. Here it is peaceful and pretty among the long grass, bog life and open views. This is my favourite **picnic stop**.

5 To continue the walk, keep ahead until you reach a metal gate. Climb the gate and proceed to a marker post leading you right as you take the final stretch of the walk. Keep to the grassy track back to the car park.

At point 4 of the walk.

◆ Background Notes ◆

Crowle Moor is owned and managed by Lincolnshire Wildlife Trust and Natural England. It is part of the remnants of the extensive wetland which occupied the flood plain of the Humberhead Levels several thousand years ago. The Humberland Peatland is still the largest area of low-level raised bog in Britain. The moors are an important conservation area for insects such as the large heath butterfly and for breeding birds, including nightingales and nightjars.

MAKING THE MOST OF YOUR DAY
- **Normanby Hall & Country Park**, 4 miles north of Scunthorpe. www.visitnorthlincolnshire.com Open from April to September.
- **Pink Pig Farm**, just south of Scunthorpe. Animals, trails, play areas and water play. www.pinkpigfarm.co.uk
- **Appleby Frodingham Railway Preservation Society**, on the eastern edge of Scunthorpe. Steam train rides. Booking essential. www.afrps.co.uk

3

Laughton Forest

Tuetoes Wood, Wonders and Wildlife

The path on the edge of the forest.

L aughton Forest in North Lincolnshire will amaze you with its towering pine trees. It sits in a picturesque area surrounded by arable and livestock farms. The route leads down a beautiful tree-lined avenue in a deciduous part of the forest and explores a stunning nature area which comes alive in the summer with butterflies and giant dragonflies. It is wonderfully shady, which makes it a good choice for a hot summer's day.

Kiddiwalks in Lincolnshire

3

 Getting there *Laughton Forest lies between Scunthorpe and Gainsborough. To reach it, head towards Laughton village and follow East Ferry Road north of the village. Towards the end of this road you will see a sign for Laughton Forest on your right. It can also be reached from Scotter, by taking the Scotterthorpe road, then the Susworth road until you pass the forest on your left. Turn left prior to Susworth.*

Length of walk 2¾ miles.
Time 1½ hours.
Terrain Flat, even terrain. Only some parts of the forest are suitable for bikes and off-road pushchairs (such as the tree-lined avenue).
Dogs No restrictions. Keep dogs under control.
Start/Parking Free car park at Laughton Forest. (GR SE846009).
Map OS Explorer 280 Isle of Axholme.

The Walk

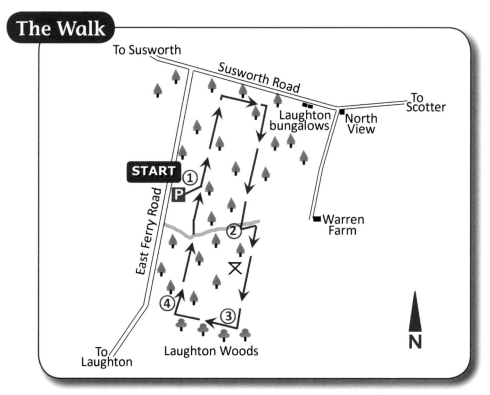

Laughton Forest

Refreshments The nearest facilities are at Blyton or Scotter, so pack a picnic to enjoy at point 2 of the walk.

1 From the car park, head into the woods between two yellow posts and a bench. Continue ahead following the woodland path. At a T-junction turn left at the red marker post. Enjoy the views of the majestic Scots and Corsican pine trees planted in 1927. At the next crossroads, continue towards the edge of the forest where there is a T-junction and a fence. Turn right. On your left you can see newly-planted trees. Continue to a main bridleway. You will see a path on the right leading into the woods.

Follow this to a crossroads and go straight on.

2 At the end of this path, you reach a sandy ditch on the right which you should be able to cross easily. If you are struggling, turn right and follow it round to the other side instead. Over the ditch, turn left and follow the overgrown track towards the edge of the woods, then turn right. From here you can see Warren Farm on your left. Continue along the fence towards the older part of the wood. As you enter the woods, continue ahead. In this section of woods there are lots of sheltered areas which make ideal **picnic spots**. You should be able to find some fallen logs for seats.

◆ Fun Things to See and Do ◆

Den Building. In the wood there are always lots of branches lying around. To make a great tree den, position it close to other trees for support. Once you get the frame right, the rest comes easily. Try using the guide on 'How to make a Survival Shelter' activity sheet on www.wildlifewatch.org.uk if you need some help.

Tree Spying Using an old unbreakable mirror, show the children how to stand underneath a tree with the mirror across their nose bridge and look down on it. As they walk very slowly around, they can see the animal and bird activity happening in the branches above.

Kiddiwalks in Lincolnshire

3 Leaving the pine woods you enter an open clearing. Continue, re-entering the deciduous forest and turn right. This section now turns into a tree-lined avenue. At the end of the path, turn right by the red marker post.

The towering pine trees near the start of the route.

4 This next section of walk has an abundance of butterflies and dragonflies in the summer. Encourage your children to hold out their hands, as the large dragonflies sometimes like to perch there. At the end of this path, at the fork, continue along the main track back into the pine forest then take the first path on the left leading through the forest. Follow this path and turn left again (about 10 m from a red post) back to the car park.

◆ Background Notes ◆

Laughton Forest was originally planted by the Forestry Commission in 1927 on an exposed hill. Before this, it was mainly open heathland and shifting sand dunes. A steady planting programme followed, with the last main planting in 1976 after freak gales devastated 400 acres of forest.

Most of Laughton Forest is leased from the Meynell Estate and public access is restricted. However, in Tuetoes Wood, which is owned by the Forestry Commission, you are welcome to explore.

The forest supports a large range of habitats and wildlife, much of which can be seen during your walk. In the summer, you can see many butterflies and dragonflies and in other parts of the wood you can look out for herons and nightjars.

MAKING THE MOST OF YOUR DAY

- **Wetlands Animal Park,** north of Retford. Lots of animals to meet here. www.wetlandsanimalpark.co.uk
- **Bransby Home of Rest for Horses,** east of Retford. Meet the retired horses; refreshments and picnic areas available. www.bransbyhorses.co.uk
- **Gainsborough Old Hall.** Medieval manor house owned by English Heritage. www.gainsboroughholdhall.co.uk
- **Gainsborough Model Railway.** For all train enthusiasts, this replica of parts of the East Coast main line from Leeds to King's Cross is one of the largest model railways in the country. It has specified opening days. www.gainsboroughmodelrailway.co.uk

Donna Nook

Seals, Shelters and Sand

Where's the sea?

This easy walk offers the chance to explore the marshland of the east coast, with all its little secrets. There are very few places like Donna Nook which offers the excitement of fast jets practising their low flying beside you and the thrill of discovering a hidden Second World War bunker and pillbox. In winter, you can even get close to thousands of breeding grey seals which bask close to the shoreline.

Donna Nook

Getting there *Donna Nook lies between Cleethorpes and Mablethorpe. From the A1031, follow signs for RAF Donna Nook by North Somercotes. Once on the road towards the beach, drive past the turning on the right for RAF Donna Nook, and continue instead to the car park at the end of the road.*

Length of walk 2 miles.
Time Allow 1½ hours.
Terrain Flat, easy terrain. Not suitable for pushchairs or bikes. Wellies are recommended.
Dogs Dog to be kept under control and off the marshland.

Start/Parking Free nature reserve car park. (GR TF422998).
Map OS Explorer 283 Louth and Mablethorpe.
Refreshments The New Inn at Saltfleetby offers good family refreshments and there is a fine picnic spot at point 4 of the walk.

1 Facing the car park noticeboard, turn left and follow the public footpath. As you walk along this grassy trail, the path bears right towards the marshland and continues ahead. This is the best place to watch the RAF practising bombing dives.

2 The path begins to merge with a track on the sandbank.

The Walk

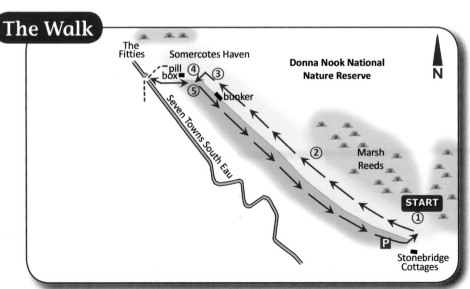

Kiddiwalks in Lincolnshire

This area can be quite muddy underfoot, but further up you can walk on the grassy bank. You can often find jellyfish washed up along this section of the walk.

3 The end of this area is marked by a white pole flying a red flag. Turn left here, climbing up the grassy bank and follow the path through, leading you over the embankment and onto a farm track. Turn right and follow the track.

4 Almost immediately to your right is a Second World

War pillbox which the children will enjoy exploring. Continue along this track towards an area called Somercotes Haven where you will see an estuary. Here is my favourite **picnic spot**. The children will enjoy exploring the estuary with its stone walls and steep steps. On the other side of the bank, the estuary continues. We now turn back and head along the farm track, passing the pillbox again.

5 Approximately 50 m ahead is a real treat for the kids as we find an underground bunker to explore. You will need a torch to

◆ Fun Things to See and Do ◆

Write up a **nature sheet** with things on it for a child to look out for and mark off. The list could include jellyfish, crab, bird feather, millipede, dragonfly, hare, grey seal and estuary.

With the Second World War element very much alive here, bring toy guns and torches and let them make up their own **war defence story** involving the bunker and pillbox.

If you are lucky you can also see the **fast jets flying overhead**, as they swoop down to bomb the planted targets out in the mudflats. They fly loud and low and are great fun to watch. Think *Top Gun!*

Grey seals bask on this coast very close to the shoreline. They gather here from the end of October to the end of December and attract up to 40,000 visitors a year.

get the most out of this one. It's worth using this area as a rest-stop so children can spend time exploring the pillbox and bunker. Once you have finished, continue back down the farm track towards the car park. This is a great place to see dragonflies. Ask the children to hold out their hands to see if one perches on them. If you prefer a change of scenery (or you want to watch the jets) climb back up the embankment where it begins to gets very bushy, which will give you a pretty walk back to the car park.

◆ Background Notes ◆

During the Second World War, **RAF Donna Nook** was significant as a radar station, spotting low-flying intruders and German E-boats cruising offshore. The bunker and pillbox remain and can be explored. In 2002, Donna Nook became the first nature reserve on Ministry of Defence land in the UK and is now managed by the Lincolnshire Wildlife Trust.

Today, Donna Nook is the east coast's bombing range and is used by many RAF bases and NATO war planes for bombing practice. You can watch video clips of the jets on YouTube if you happen to miss the real thing.

Just as significant is the **grey seal colony** which returns every year to breed. There are usually over 3,000 seals lining the shore from late October to the end of December, attracting thousands of visitors who can watch the new pups at very close range.

MAKING THE MOST OF YOUR DAY
- **Oasis Lakes, North Somercotes.** This is a beautiful lake and professional fishery. You can hire rods and spend some time fishing. www.oasislakes.co.uk
- **Howdens Pullover.** This is a beauty spot signposted south of North Somercotes. It makes for a good picnic spot, particularly when the tide is in.
- **Mablethorpe.** This 1950s coastal resort lies 8 miles to the south and offers all the fun of the seaside, as well as a long promenade to meander down.

5

Willingham Woods

The English Rainforest

Willingham Ponds.

Willingham Woods is a popular stopping-off point for those travelling along the A631 outside Market Rasen. The woods resemble a rainforest, which makes it very endearing. On this woodland walk, we explore a small circular section, deemed to be the best 'starter' route.

Getting there *Willingham Woods is well signposted off the A631 east of Market Rasen.*

Length of walk 2 miles.
Time Allow 1½ hours.
Terrain Uneven in places so not recommended for pushchairs. Suitable for mountain bikes, though can be muddy underfoot in some areas.
Dogs No restrictions. Keep dogs under control.
Start/Parking Free car park at Willingham Woods. Drive through the parking bay area by the snack hut to the far end where there is a separate car park by the large green picnic area. (GR TF138884).
Map OS Explorer 282 Lincolnshire Wolds North.

Refreshments There is a popular café hut on site serving bacon baps, burgers and drinks. Picnic tables and toilets are also available at the picnic site. Another good picnic spot can be found at point 3 of the walk.

1 From the information board by the picnic area, turn left and follow the main track through the woods. On the left are dark wooded areas, fun for children to dart in and out of. Continue until you reach five wooden posts at the end of the trail. Turn right.

2 This path takes you deeper into the woods and is quite dark and dense. It is a fun place for children to run around between the trees and explore, while still being visible. Ahead, the path

The Walk

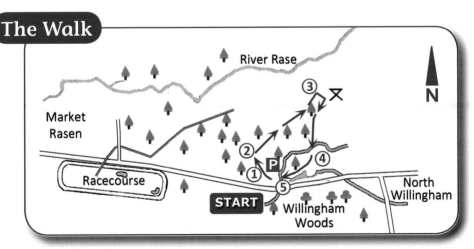

Kiddiwalks in Lincolnshire

joins a crossroads but you remain ahead all the way until you reach the end of the wood. Do not turn right where you see a red marker post, instead go ahead where there is a red and white marker post.

3 This section can be muddy underfoot after wet weather. At the edge of the wood, the path bears to the right with ferns either side. Follow the path and you will immediately see to your left an opening into a field. Go through this gap if you want to enjoy what is my favourite **picnic stop**. It is advisable to bring a blanket in case the ground is damp. It is very quiet and pleasant, with an open field where the children can play freely. It's time for you to grab your flask and enjoy the country views! Once you are ready, go back into the woods and follow the path left which circumnavigates the edge of the wood. This is a very pretty, winding path with many ferns framing the way. At the end of the path where it forks, bear left towards the post with the red and white marker and cross the brick bridge.

4 After crossing the bridge, bear right. You will pass a stream on your right. There are often small trails cutting through your path, but you should stick to the main graded path. Eventually, you will reach a post with a red marker at a fork. Bear left and at the end of the path you come to a T-junction, bear left. At the end of this path, turn right through the woodland.

5 You are nearing the end of your walk as you reach Willingham Ponds with many resident ducks and moorhens. There are two picnic tables here but although the setting

◆ Fun Things to See and Do ◆

Play **'Follow the Leader'** through the dark and dense part of the woods. Remember to bring some bread to **feed the ducks**. The large green area by the car park is perfect for **ball games**. Children passing through often join in games of football, cricket or rounders.

is pretty, there can be traffic noise from the A631. (If you have a dog, you should put it on a lead.) The main pond is clear water, but the other, which is bound to attract your hound, is very muddy – shockingly so! Once you've enjoyed the ducks, continue along this path which leads back to the main picnic area and car park.

A good spot for a picnic.

◆ Background Notes ◆

Market Rasen was described by Charles Dickens as 'the sleepiest town in England'. Today it is a small market town where the biggest economy is agriculture. This quiet town did hit the headlines in 2008, however, when it was the centre of an earthquake measuring 5.2 on the Richter scale! Market Rasen now has Lincolnshire's only racecourse. Various fixtures and meetings all year round. For race details contact www.marketrasenraces.co.uk

MAKING THE MOST OF YOUR DAY
- **Cadwell Park Motor Racing Circuit**, south-west of Louth on the A153. Great fun to watch. Under 13s are often admitted free. www.cadwellpark.org.uk
- **Goltho Gardens.** South of Market Rasen on the A158, west of Wragby. An established 4½-acre garden with lovely pathways to explore, including the Nut Walk. Toilets and parking available. www.golthogardens.com

Hubbard's Hills

A Victorian Love Story

The River Lud flows through Hubbard's Hills.

'As a child, this was a truly enchanting place to visit, that will stay in my mind forever' so says local historian, John Pinchbeck. Many people from Louth, in fact, speak very affectionately of this park. It's one of the rare beauties which captures the elegance of times gone by for there is something very endearing and old-fashioned about it. This is a short walk, which follows the river path, the open hills and the cliff ridge.

Hubbard's Hills

Getting there *Hubbard's Hills is on the western edge of Louth. To find the main car park on Crowtree Lane, follow the B1200 from its junction with the A157 towards Louth. Turn right at the Elkington roundabout following the signs to Louth town centre. Turn right into Love Lane, then right again into Crowtree Lane. Continue until you reach the car park at the end of the single track road. (There is another car park on Halfpenny Lane at the southern end of Hubbard's Hills off the Horncastle Road.)*

Length of walk 1½ miles.

Time Allow 1 hour.

Terrain The river path section is flat and easy so is suitable for pushchairs and bikes. The route gets very hilly as you climb up to the ridge, though, and there is a moderately steep climb to the hills.

Dogs Dogs must be on leads in parts of the park but are allowed off the lead in some marked areas.

Start/Parking Crowtree Lane car park where a small fee is payable. (GR TF316867).

Map OS Explorer 282 Lincolnshire Wolds North.

Refreshments A small café at the car park sells snacks, ice-cream and drinks. Picnic tables are available in the children's play area. My favourite picnic spot is at point 4 of the walk.

❶ From the toilet block in the Crowtree Lane car park, turn right and follow the path along the riverside. Here you will see dozens of ducks so make sure you take some bread so the children can feed them. Continue along

◆ Fun Things to See and Do ◆

Feed the **ducks**. Use the swings and climbing frame in the **play area**. Climb the steep banks. Cross the stepping stones, use your fishing net to go **pond dipping**, **paddle** in the shallow water, **sail** your toy boat. Remember to bring a swim suit, towel and waterproof shoes (just in case!).

Kiddiwalks in Lincolnshire

The Walk

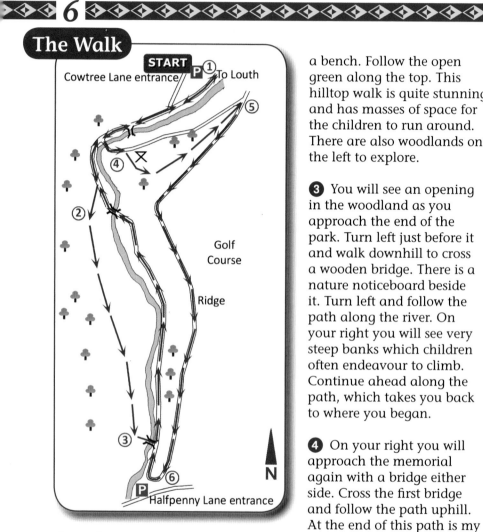

a bench. Follow the open green along the top. This hilltop walk is quite stunning and has masses of space for the children to run around. There are also woodlands on the left to explore.

❸ You will see an opening in the woodland as you approach the end of the park. Turn left just before it and walk downhill to cross a wooden bridge. There is a nature noticeboard beside it. Turn left and follow the path along the river. On your right you will see very steep banks which children often endeavour to climb. Continue ahead along the path, which takes you back to where you began.

❹ On your right you will approach the memorial again with a bridge either side. Cross the first bridge and follow the path uphill. At the end of this path is my favourite **picnic spot**, an open green area high above the river with lovely views. Continue up towards the ridge. From this green bank, walk north-east towards a path leading uphill. There is a green rail to assist you with the steep climb.

the path past two sets of stepping stones and a memorial. From here you will see a 'dogs roaming free' sign and a hill on your right-hand side.

❷ Release the hound if you have one, and climb the hill towards

5 Once at the top, turn right and follow the ridge path which is very high in places and follows the golf course on your left.

6 At the end, turn right and follow the steps down to the Halfpenny Lane entrance. Turn right and retrace your steps through the park along the river towards the Crowtree Lane entrance. You may want to while away your time and sit by the river near the stepping stones. It is a very popular spot and children love to play in this shallow part of the river. This is definitely my favourite place to spend the rest of the day!

◆ Background Notes ◆

A Victorian love story began in 1875 when a Swiss teacher, Auguste Alphonse Pahud, arrived in Louth to teach French to the boys at the local grammar school. He met and fell in love with Annie Grant, daughter of a wealthy farmer. The couple married and became inseparable. When Annie died in 1899, Auguste was inconsolable and became a hermit until his death less than three years later. In his will he left instructions for a board of trustees to be set up to distribute his fortune to celebrate the memory of his wife. Hubbard's Hills was bought and developed as a lasting memorial to his beloved Annie. On 3 August 1907 there were great celebrations as Hubbard's Hills were given to the people of Louth.

MAKING THE MOST OF YOUR DAY

- **Northcote Heavy Horse Centre**, near Spilsby is a non-profit-making organisation run by volunteers providing a care home for horses. www.northcotehorses.com
- **Radcliffe Donkey Sanctuary**, near Alford. Free entry to a 30-acre site for donkeys. Feed the donkeys, refreshments available. www.radcliffedonkeys.com
- **Hedgehog Care**, Authorpe. This is a hedgehog hospital where visitors are able to take a peep at patients and buy gifts and 'Hogsfarm' clothes in the shop. www.hedgehogcare.org.uk

Saltfleetby-Theddlethorpe Dunes

The Seaview Trail

On the path beside the marshes.

Saltfleetby-Theddlethorpe is a beautiful coastal reserve. For children who live inland, coming out to the coast at any time of the year is a real treat. It offers a completely different Lincolnshire landscape. There are sand dunes to climb, ponds to observe and marshes to meander by. There are several trails to follow on the reserve, leaving from different car parks. Our route follows the varied Seaview Trail and those with pushchairs or wheelchairs can take the Rimac Trail, which has paths laid specially to accommodate them.

Saltfleetby-Theddlethorpe Dunes

Getting there *Travel south from Saltfleet on the A1031 and follow the brown tourism sign for the car park at Sea View Farm.*

Length of walk 2 miles.
Time Allow 2 hours.
Terrain This walk is not suitable for pushchairs unless you take the shorter Rimac Trail which starts from the Rimac car park between points 3 and 5. (GR TF468918).
Dogs Dogs to be under control.

Start/Parking The Sea View Farm free car park. (GR TF465924).
Map OS Explorer 283 Louth & Mablethorpe.
Refreshments The nearest facilities are in Saltfleet. There is a possible picnic spot in a meadow after point 6.

1 It should be noted that there are several colour-coded walks around the reserve. However, over time the markers have faded and it is very difficult to distinguish between them. There are three pathways from the Seaview Farm car park. Take the path at the rear, beside the farm, and follow the small grassy trail which takes you along the edge of Sea View Farm. At the end of the path you reach a small wooden gate. Go through the gate, turn right and follow the edge of the field. As you loop round, you will see a post with an arrow on it. Follow the field round to the left where you see a second post directing you right by the public footpath sign.

The Walk

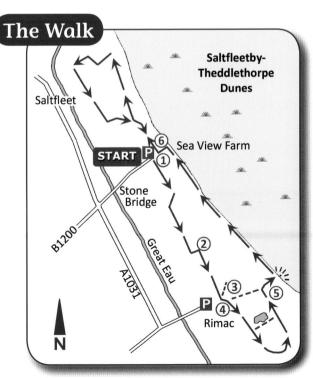

Saltfleet

Saltfleetby-Theddlethorpe Dunes

Sea View Farm

START P ①

⑥ P

Stone Bridge

B1200

Great Eau

A1031

②

③

⑤

P ④

Rimac

N

Kiddiwalks in Lincolnshire

2 Here you walk alongside a field that may contain livestock to a wooden gate at the end.

3 Before you leave this field, climb the wooden steps to the viewpoint on your left where there is also a bench.

4 After visiting the viewpoint go through the wooden gate. Cross the path in front of you to the second path and follow this. If you want to linger, there is a pond on your left with a viewing platform, and a higher viewpoint on your right. Many butterflies and dragonflies can be found in this area, and bilberries in season. Continue along the path until it bears left and loops back round past the pond. At the noticeboard between the dunes, continue ahead.

5 Now turn right at the crossroads towards the sign about the tide. Follow the marked path to the viewpoint. After taking in the view, continue your walk by returning down the path to an unmarked path beside it leading towards the marshland. Turn left onto the public footpath and continue along this grassy path past high reeds and marshland back to the car park. This section can seem quite long, so ask the children to look out for different birds such as skylark, redshank, linnet and geese, until you reach a marked post which leads left into the car park.

6 Don't go into the car park but take the second left instead, which bypasses the car park and leads you straight to the Meadow Loop (1 km). Walk up the hill

◆ Fun Things to See and Do ◆

Nature Quiz. Try www.outdoor-nature-child.com for inspirational questions. Children love being tested and will learn facts too. Take binoculars to use at the viewpoints. From May to October you can see migrating **birds**. Keep your eyes open for old **wartime gun posts** and the body of an **old tank**.

towards a pillbox and turn right. Continue ahead and go through a wooden gate. Follow the arrows which loop you round the meadow. There are many small trails here which the children will enjoy running up and down. Don't leave the meadow to go into the next field, as the path only goes ahead. Once you have looped round, head back to the car park.

The view over the reserve.

◆ Background Notes ◆

Saltfleetby-Theddlethorpe Dunes Nature Reserve is managed by Natural England. The dunes were commonly used by smugglers in the 18th and 19th centuries to hide their booty which included gin, tobacco, and sometimes wool. It was often the site for shipwrecks too.

The dunes were purchased in the mid 1930s by the Air Ministry for use as a bombing range. Today an old tank can be seen which was used for target practice.

MAKING THE MOST OF YOUR DAY

- **Mablethorpe Seafront.** Visit Queen's Park, walk along the long seafront or even cycle it out of season. Funfair, donkey rides and sand train.
- **Alford.** Pretty, ancient market town, with a market on Tuesdays. Lots of small shops and tearooms. Also **Alford Manor House** www.alfordmanorhouse.co.uk and **Alford Five Sailed Windmill.**
- **Claythorpe Watermill and Wildfowl Gardens.** A watermill in a picture-postcard setting, enchanted woods and tearoom. www.claythorpewatermill.fsbusiness.co.uk

8

Chambers Farm Wood

The Red Trail

The Butterfly Garden on the edge of the wood.

Chambers Farm Wood is part of the Bardney Limewoods National Nature Reserve. It sits 11 miles east of Lincoln. This ancient wood has marked easy trails and makes for a very pleasant day out. There are picnic tables and the added attraction of a beautiful dedicated butterfly garden to explore.

Chambers Farm Wood

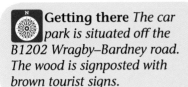 **Getting there** *The car park is situated off the B1202 Wragby–Bardney road. The wood is signposted with brown tourist signs.*

Length of walk 2½ miles.
Time Allow 2 hours.
Terrain Flat, easy terrain, so good for pushchairs and bikes.
Dogs No restrictions. Keep dogs under control.
Start/Parking The free car park at the wood. (GR TF148738).

Map OS Explorer 273 Lincolnshire Wolds South.
Refreshments None but ideal for a picnic at the tables on site. Toilets are available near the Butterfly Garden.

❶ From the car park, take the Dog Walkers' Path. This goes along a woodland trail.

❷ At the end, where you meet a path, turn right. Follow the path round and stay right. At the end you will meet a main path – the

The Walk

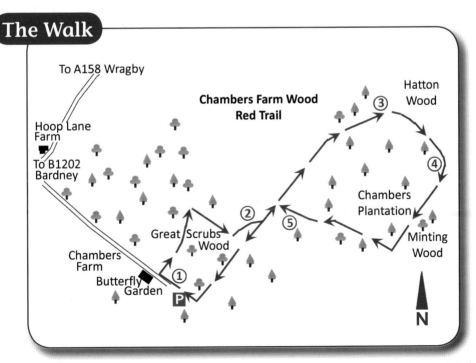

Kiddiwalks in Lincolnshire

Red Trail. Turn left to follow it. This is a flat path and very easy to follow. The first section is straight, with forest on both sides – ideal for the children to dart in and out of. When you reach the bench at the junction, you may wish to take a rest. It is the only bench on the route. Continue, keeping left. The walk then takes a more interesting and enclosed appearance. If you want a more secluded rest, further up there is a circular space on your right which is fine for sitting down on a rug. It is just after a footpath leading off to the left.

3 Follow the path all the way round. It eventually curves towards Hatton Woods, which is home to rare barbastelle bats. You will notice another path leading left. Ignore it, unless you are feeling adventurous and want to explore deeper inside the woods (although it is very pretty, it is not suitable for pushchairs). To stay on the Red Trail look for a red marker ahead, leading you right.

4 You now walk alongside Minting Wood, again home of bats. Bear right at a junction and continue back to the bench at point 3.

5 Turn left and follow the red markers back to the car park. Don't forget to pay a visit to the Butterfly Garden by the toilet and information block.

◆ Fun Things to See and Do ◆

Scavenger Hunt Use a decorated egg box to collect pieces found on the walk e.g. different coloured leaves, different types of feathers and different grasses. These can be used to make a picture.

Butterfly Hunt In spring and summer there are lots of butterflies in this wood. Bring a butterfly species guide and use it to see how many types you can identify. Pretend that butterflies are really fairies in disguise, the prettiest of which is the Fairy Queen. www.naturedetectives.org.uk

Exploring the fields.

◆ Background Notes ◆

Chambers Farm Wood is owned by the Forestry Commission. It lies in the heart of the Lincolnshire Limewoods and is one of the largest woodlands to be part of the Bardney Limewoods National Nature Reserve. The trails hold clues to the rich and varied past of this ancient area from the time of the Domesday Book.

MAKING THE MOST OF YOUR DAY

- **Mrs Smith's Cottage**, Navenby. A cottage in a 1920s time-warp, now a museum open to visitors. www.mrssmithscottage.co.uk
- **Wragby Maze and Conifer Centre.** Get lost in the Hedge Maze! Also outdoor games, refreshments and a picnic site. www.amazing-conifers.com

9

Hartsholme Country Park

Hidden in the City

Hartsholme Lake.

Hartsholme Country Park is an oasis of countryside on the outskirts of the city of Lincoln. This walk, with its marked paths, woodland, meadows and lakes, makes for a lovely day out all year round. Swanholme Lakes is a local nature reserve that can be reached through the country park and there are plenty of picnic spots, a children's adventure playground and a campsite.

Getting there *The country park is signposted from the A46 west of Lincoln at the Skellingthorpe roundabout. The entrance is on the B1378 Skellingthorpe road.*

Length of walk 2¾ miles.
Time Allow 2 hours.
Terrain Flat and even. Pushchair

and cycle-friendly all the way round.
Dogs Keep dogs under control. Dogs on leads in Swanholme Nature Reserve.
Start/Parking There is free car parking at the country park. (GR SK946696).
Map OS Explorer 272 Lincoln.
Refreshments Toilets and good refreshments are available at the visitor centre and café which serves hot lunches and children's meals. There are also picnic spots along the way.

The Walk

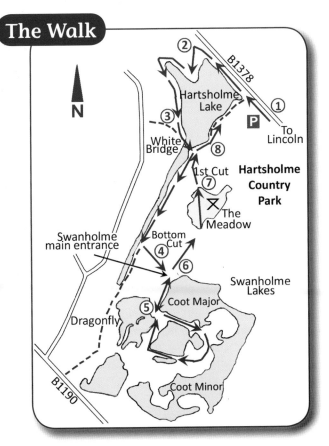

❶ From the car park, walk towards the main entrance and turn left onto a path parallel to the main road. Follow the path as it takes you along Hartsholme Lake. Continue to the end and turn left.

❷ The lake should be on your left as you walk through the woods. Further along, the path breaks into a fork. Bear left by the bench.

43

3 Cross the first bridge known as White Bridge, then turn right and follow the path. The lake is on your right. You will pass two openings into the woods as you follow the path. Take the third opening marked 'Bottom Cut Through' on your left and cross the small footbridge.

4 The trail through the woods forks. Bear right and head towards a large gate signposted 'Swanholme Lakes Local Nature Reserve'. Go through the gate and follow the path until you see a single-storey green building.

5 Take the left path here and follow the circular route around the lake. On your left is Coot Major and on your right is The Sanctuary, an area for swans. A few metres down the path there is a bench close to a good **picnic spot**. As you come towards the end of the route around the sanctuary, you reach a T-junction. Turn right, back to the green building, then bear left back to the main gate.

6 From this gate turn right and follow the path through the woods. Continue along this woodland path until you reach a double wooden gate on your left. Go through the gate to The Meadow, another ideal **picnic spot** with several picnic benches and space for children to play. Follow the path ahead that bears left. The tree-line should be on your left

◆ Fun Things to See and Do ◆

The Swanholme Lakes local nature reserve is still undergoing planting. The reserve is home to plenty of wildlife with many ducks and swans on the lakes. **Special food to feed the ducks** can be purchased from the visitor centre as they want to discourage the use of bread. The woodland is home to many wild birds and squirrels.
Scavenger Hunt – as this walk meanders through the medley of water, woods and meadows, this can make an interesting scavenger hunt. Give your child a small basket or bag and ask them to collect five different leaves, one empty snail shell, two different feathers, one fir cone, one nut, two different seeds and three different types of grass.

as you walk towards the first bench. Just before you reach the bench, bear right, following the pathway across the meadows towards the woods. At the end of the meadow the path bears left through the woods.

7 Follow the trail through the woods. You reach a small wooden footbridge marked 'First Cut Through'. Turn right, back to the main riverside path. Follow the path through to the left where

you will see the White Bridge. Continue by the boathouse, bearing left and follow the river.

8 Walk along the river's edge until you reach the former site of Hartsholme Hall. Here are some totem poles and a raised area reached by steps. Take the second set of steps on your right and continue to the play area on your left. Follow the path until you see a sign directing you back to the visitor centre and toilets.

◆ Background Notes ◆

Hartsholme Lake was constructed in 1848 by the Lincoln Waterworks Company to provide water for 733 houses. Hartsholme Hall was built around 1862 for Joseph Shuttleworth. During the Second World War, the estate was used for military purposes. After the war, the hall suffered neglect, vandalism, damage and theft and in 1947 it became home to 32 squatter families. It was eventually demolished in 1951 and the park was opened to the public. Hartsholme has been a country park since 1974.

MAKING THE MOST OF YOUR DAY
- **Daisy Made, Skellingthorpe.** This is a drive-through ice-cream parlour and café with the best home-made ice creams, created on the dairy farm. It also has a play area, mini golf, a bouncy castle and animals to see. www.daisymadeicecream.co.uk
- **Bransby Home of Rest for Horses**, north-west of Lincoln off the A1500. Meet the horses, enjoy refreshments or just picnic here. www.bransbyhorses.co.uk
- **Doddington Hall & Gardens**, 3 miles west of the country park. This stately home offers beautiful gardens including a turf maze, a farm shop, and a café. www.doddingtonhall.com

10

Whisby Nature Park

Magpie Walk

Time for reflection.

Whisby Nature Park makes a great family day out. There are stunning peaceful walks in beautiful lakeside and woodland settings and a wonderful play area – Little Darters Wildlife Adventure Area – with sand pit, water play, cave, pontoon and a hide. The whole outing makes for a great childhood adventure.

Whisby Nature Park

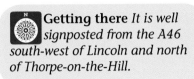

Getting there *It is well signposted from the A46 south-west of Lincoln and north of Thorpe-on-the-Hill.*

Length of walk 2½ miles.
Time Allow 1½ hours.
Terrain Pushchair- and cycle-friendly all the way round.
Dogs Keep dogs on a lead.

Start/Parking The visitor centre car park where a small fee is payable. (GR SK914662)
Map OS Explorer 272 Lincoln.
Refreshments There is a self-service café and snack hut, with plenty of picnic tables.

The Walk

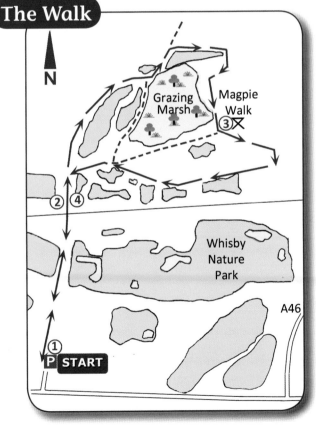

❶ From the visitor centre, turn left and follow the path that leads down towards the lakeside. The Magpie Walk, like all the reserve walks, is waymarked very clearly all the way round. It follows the green arrows, beginning with a lakeside walk with plenty of benches for scenic rests. The walk curves to a railway bridge, where children can enjoy watching trains from the footbridge.

❷ The Magpie Walk takes you through a section of shady woodland through willow and birch woods. Keep an eye out for the posts marking hides, the children will enjoy creeping into these and watching the wildlife.

47

Kiddiwalks in Lincolnshire

Enjoying an evening swim.

◆ Fun Things to See and Do ◆

This is a very beautiful reserve. Encourage your children to bring some paper, crayons, paints or pencils and sit on one of the trail benches with a view so they can **enjoy being an artist**. This will help children see their environment in a different way, looking more carefully at the colours and shapes around them. **Explore the hides** in a top secret mission. Explain to the children that to cross through to the animal hide you have to pretend to be special soldiers on a covert operation, keeping low, being very quiet and blending in with the environment. Once in the hide their mission is to use their binoculars to spot approaching animals and birds and noting them down.

3 My **favourite picnic spot** is marked at post M7, where there is a single bench. This lovely peaceful spot is the halfway mark.

4 The remainder of the walk follows grazing marsh and crosses back over the railway bridge to the visitor centre.

◆ Background Notes ◆

Whisby Nature Reserve is one of the county's principal reserves. Opened in 1989, it is managed by the Lincolnshire Wildlife Trust in partnership with the local and district councils. It consists of 150 hectares of wetland, grassland and scrub habitat. The extensive lakes are the result of sand and gravel extraction. There is an Education Centre and exhibitions in the Natural World Centre. www.lincstrust.org.uk

MAKING THE MOST OF YOUR DAY

- **Daisy Made, Skellingthorpe.** This is a drive-through ice-cream parlour and café with the best home-made ice creams, created on the dairy farm. It also has a play area, mini golf, a bouncy castle and animals to see. www.daisymadeicecream.co.uk
- **Pennell's Garden Centre** (at the A46 roundabout, just east of Thorpe-on-the-Hill). More than just a garden centre. www.pennellsonline.co.uk
- **The Gamekeeper** (at the same A46 roundabout). Family pub with meal deals and indoor and outdoor play areas.

11

Snipe Dales Round

Hills of the Wolds

Along the way.

S nipe Dales is one of the gems of the Lincolnshire Wolds. It lies near Horncastle and contradicts the 'Lincolnshire is flat' myth. It is a beautiful country park with a nature reserve that takes on a hilly and winding exterior. It makes for a great adventure as there are several marked trails to follow for all abilities. In the spring and summer, the reserve is particularly stunning.

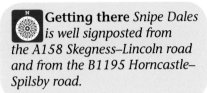

Getting there *Snipe Dales is well signposted from the A158 Skegness–Lincoln road and from the B1195 Horncastle–Spilsby road.*

Length of walk 3½ miles.
Time Allow 2 hours.
Terrain Hilly in places. An off-road pushchair may cope on some paths, but are not generally recommended for this walk.
Dogs Dogs only allowed in the country park. They are not permitted in the nature reserve or the picnic area.
Start/Parking The country park car park where a small fee is payable.
Map OS Explorer 273 Lincolnshire Wolds South (GR TF330682).

Refreshments None available on the route but picnic tables are available throughout and nearby Horncastle offers lots of choice. There are toilets in the car park.

1 This trail is very clearly marked all the way round with red marker posts. From the picnic area near the car park, walk to the start point for the trail and follow the red marker posts for the Snipe Dales Round trail. There are shorter trails to follow if you wish. However, this trail is the only one which takes in the nature reserve. The trail starts by going downhill, where a picnic table is sited.

2 Follow the red trail which veers left and makes its way up towards the woodland. Encourage

The Walk

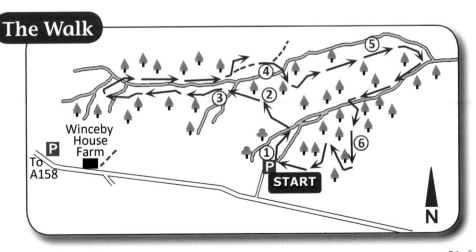

Winceby House Farm

To A158

P

START

N

In the reserve.

◆ Fun Things to See and Do ◆

Sleeping Lions: Lie down in the long grass of the nature reserve, shut your eyes and see if you can identify ten different nature sounds, such as bird calls, insects, mice and other animals rustling. See who can stay the quietest for longest.

Elf tracking: This is good if there are several children and adults in the party. An adult goes ahead and lays a track using twigs, leaves and stones, for the children to follow. The 'elves' have left this trail for them which leads them to their secret place.

the children to hunt out the markers on the trail.

3 After leaving the top of the woodland you enter the nature reserve and loop around it. This is particularly stunning in summer and makes for a lovely place to stop. Remember that dogs are not permitted on this part of the trail.

4 Once you leave the nature reserve, you go back into the woodland, your halfway point.

5 Here you are at the lowest point of the country park. Children will enjoy running through the trees.

6 The remainder of the trail takes you back up the hill and through a pretty woodland area. There are signs leading you back to the car park.

◆ Background Notes ◆

Snipe Dales is owned by Lincolnshire Wildlife Trust. It is an area of two halves, with mixed woodland in the country park and wet valleys in the nature reserve. The woodland was planted in 1965 and the Corsican pines are gradually being replaced with ash, oak and alder trees. The nature reserve has a semi-natural, wet valley system, fretted by streams. A broad range of birds, wild flowers and insect life can been seen here. www.lincstrust.org.uk

MAKING THE MOST OF YOUR DAY
- **Horncastle.** There is a pleasant children's playground called Coronation Walk by the canal. Follow signs towards the swimming pool to find it. The town is quaint and historic, with a lovely canal walk, antique shops and tea rooms.
- **Battle of Britain Memorial Flight Visitor Centre, Coningsby,** south of Horncastle on the A153. www.lincolnshire.gov.uk/bbmf.
- **RAF Coningsby.** From Coningsby, follow the signs to the RAF station. Opposite the flight take-off is a parking area. There you can safely watch jet aircraft taking off and landing. The best times are Monday to Friday, 8 am to 5 pm. A timetable of flying can be found at www.Raf.mod.uk/rafconingsby.

Ostler's Plantation

The Dambusters' Den

Walking the heather-edged path.

Ostler's Plantation has a magical hidden secret within its lush woodland. This was an airfield during the Second World War, used by the Dambuster Squadron. During this walk you will come across taxiways and bunkers and, of course, the airfield itself. This particular route takes in the circumference of the wood. There are many weaving pathways which are not marked on any map, so feel free to explore your own routes. This wood is fenced all the way round, so you cannot stray too far.

Ostler's Plantation

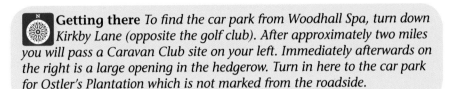
Length of walk 2½ miles.
Time Allow 2 hours.
Terrain Easy flat trails underfoot. Only parts of the wood are suitable for pushchairs and bikes.
Dogs No restrictions. Keep dogs under control.
Start/Parking Ostler's Plantation free car park. (GR TF216629).
Map OS Explorer 273 Lincolnshire Wolds South.
Refreshments None available on the route but there are two picnic tables on site. Woodhall Spa offers many amenities.

1 From the information board in the car park, take the first trail path to the right into the woods. As you follow this, you will notice the roadside to your right. At the end of this trail you will reach a small green clearing. Continue, and then turn right through the

The Walk

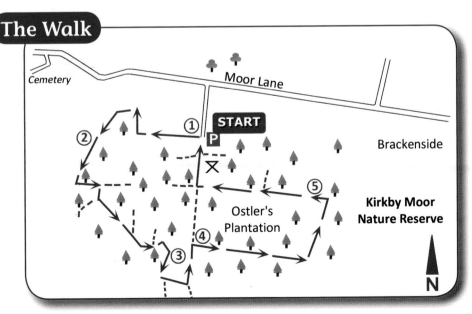

Kiddiwalks in Lincolnshire

bushes. This path will take you to the edge of the woods, parallel with the road and it curves to the left.

2 When you reach the edge of the woods, you are met with three small paths leading in different directions. Take the middle path. You will see farmland in the distance on your right. Follow the path until you approach a concrete road (part of the former airfield). Turn right and follow the outer edge of the wood. Continue for some time, passing two small separate grassy banks on your way. Eventually you reach the first path back into the woods on your left and this is surrounded by ferns. Take this path and bear right towards the road when it forks by the disused bunker.

3 Once on the road, turn right towards a brick ruin (which the children may wish to explore). Continue ahead to three disused RAF bunkers on your left. Turn left on the path towards the bunker with the red door. Walk around the back of these buildings then 60 m ahead, towards the path where you turn left. (If you go right, you will reach the edge of the woods and see extensive views of the countryside, pond and quarry.) After turning left, cross the path which becomes a wide road. Take the first right through the woods until it curves to a

◆ Fun Things to See and Do ◆

Tell the children the story of the 617 Dambuster Squadron. For information see www.Dambusters.org.uk. Once the children understand the story they may wish to re-enact it, using the bunkers and airfield strip. They could bring their own **toy aeroplanes**, or make one using card. If you have children interested in this story, there is an opportunity for them to see **jets take-off and landing at RAF Coningsby** (near Woodhall Spa). Follow signs to RAF Coningsby, and continue all the way round until you come to a dead end at the end of the airfield. You will see a lot of plane spotters parked up here. They will advise you when the jets are due to fly.

Jubilee Park is well worth a visit after your walk.

concrete road. Walk diagonally across the road until it joins a main section of road and bear left. Follow the path all the way down. You can see how the composition of the wood begins to change, with pine trees on your left and smaller trees on your right.

4 When you reach the main crossroads, turn right and follow this path to the edge of the woods. This path is sandy with heather growing alongside it. It leads you to the edge of Kirkby Moor Nature Reserve, which cannot be accessed from Ostler's Plantation (see below). If you are not planning to visit the nature reserve, this route gives you plenty of opportunity to view it from the path. As you reach the fenced edge of Kirkby Moor, the

path curves to the left and follows the outskirts of the reserve.

5 When you reach a set of large telegraph poles, turn left along the path which goes back into the woods. This is quite a long path and a good place to stop for a game or a story. There are often fallen logs here for sitting on. When you reach the first crossroads, continue ahead. As you approach the second set of crossroads further up, you will notice two picnic tables which make an ideal **picnic spot**. Turn right, and you will see the car park.

◆ Background Notes ◆

The history of the **617 Dambuster Squadron base** is very much alive here in the heart of Ostler's Plantation. Lancaster bombers flew from this airfield in 1943/45. Taxiways and bunkers are still visible through the woodland. The area itself was named after Mr Ostler who created a plantation here in the 19th century. He planted a fir and oak forest after the original forest burned down. The airfield, built in 1942, is now overgrown and unused. The wood is owned by the Forestry Commission. www.forestry.gov.uk

MAKING THE MOST OF YOUR DAY
- **Jubliee Park**, Woodhall Spa. A beautiful park created in the 1930s with traditional English gardens and a bandstand. It has a lovely play area, picnic tables, free parking, snack/ice-cream hut and an outdoor heated swimming pool. www.jubileeparkwoodhallspa.co.uk
- **Kinema in the Woods**, Woodhall Spa. This unique 1920s cinema is situated in the woods and shows both modern and black-and-white films. It is very old-fashioned and sometimes begins showings with an organist. www.thekinemainthewoods.co.uk.
- **Kirkby Moor Nature Reserve**, near Woodhall Spa. Owned by Lincolnshire Wildlife Trust www.lincstrust.org.uk/reserves. Access is a little further east along Moor Lane, opposite Wellsyke Lane.

13

Gibraltar Point

Sand Dunes and Seagulls

The beach in winter.

The biggest thrill on this walk is the opportunity for the children to get onto the beach. The walk is fantastic in any season so why limit your visit to the summer? The area includes a sandy and muddy shore, dunes, salt marsh and fresh water marsh with ponds and a lagoon and a mass of wildlife to observe. Don't forget to pack the children's buckets and spades, and why not drop in at the visitor centre afterwards? It's also worth checking the tide times (www.britishbeaches.info) before you set off as this beach is best enjoyed when the tide is not fully out.

Kiddiwalks in Lincolnshire

13

Getting there *Gibraltar Point lies 3 miles south of Skegness where the road comes to an end. It can be reached by following the brown tourism signs through the town.*

Length of walk 2 miles.
Time Allow 1½ hours.
Terrain Clear paths at the start but the beach and marshy areas will be more difficult for pushchairs.

Dogs Dogs are banned from the beach from 1 April to1 September and must be on a lead at other times.

Start/Parking The beach car park (fee payable) is the first of two car parks you reach for the reserve. (GR TF558588).

The Walk

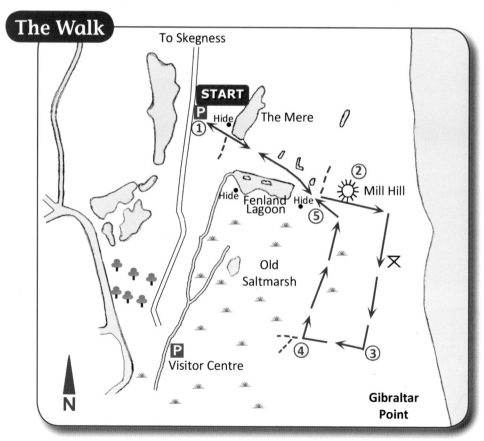

60

Map OS Explorer 274 Skegness.
Refreshments The visitor centre (at the second car park) offers toilets, a shop and a café serving hot meals and snacks. Otherwise, head into Skegness for lots of choice.

1 Leave the car park and walk through the gate into the nature reserve. On your left is an area called The Mere which is a popular spot for many varieties of birds. On your right is a field where black Hebridean sheep are often found grazing. Continue along the path until you see some steps leading up to a viewpoint called Mill Hill. This is the highest point on the reserve and is often used to watch the migration of birds. If you have a pushchair, you can walk around this, otherwise go up the steps where the children will get their first glimpse of the sea.

2 From Mill Hill go ahead towards the beach. Here there are sand dunes galore for the children to explore. As long as it's not too cold or windy, this is my favourite **picnic spot**. To continue, turn right along the beach and walk another 300 m until you see on your right the first break in the dunes. Take this sandy path to return inland.

3 This area becomes quite marshy. Be warned – if you do this walk in summer there may be a lot of flies, and in winter, wellies are required! Continue to

◆ Fun Things to See and Do ◆

Pond dipping for crabs and starfish. Use buckets and spades to make **dribble castles** (these are tall pointed Gothic-style castles) – see who can make the tallest! Or make sand faces with your spade or a stick. Children may enjoy bringing toy diggers or cars with them. **Shell collecting.** See how many different types of shells you can find. Finally, make sure you wrap up warm for this walk and wear wellies as the sea air on the east coast can be particularly fresh at most times of year. **Take a flask, sit down and enjoy the peace** – because the kids will be busy for a long time!

some steep wooden steps on your right and climb them. At the top of the steps there is a Lincolnshire Wildlife Trust map pinpointing your position. We now follow the marked wheelchair-access route.

4 Cross towards the wooden bridge and take the right turn through a gate which has a picture of cattle on it. From here you follow the path all the way back to Mill Hill. There is a bench along the path. At the end of the field is a gate. Turn left out of the gate.

5 Turn left along the path and follow the outward route back to the car park.

◆ Background Notes ◆

Gibraltar Point National Nature Reserve covers 1,000 acres along three miles of coastline from Skegness to The Wash. Gibraltar Point was once a busy port. Its steady decline and the build-up of sand dunes eventually left the place deserted by 1925. In 1948, the Lincolnshire Wildlife Trust took over management of the 1,000-acre site after plans for it to become a speedway circuit were rejected.

The reserve has steadily developed over time with a new visitor centre, marked pathways and the development of new meres and ponds. If you haven't been there for a while – it's definitely worth revisiting. It is recognised internationally as an area of outstanding wildlife and geomorphological importance. It has also been designated a Site of Special Scientific Interest (SSSI). It is particularly interesting to watch the migrating birds so make sure you bring along your binoculars.

MAKING THE MOST OF YOUR DAY
- **Skegness.** You just have to stop on your way back through. It is the closest thing to Blackpool on the east coast. A bustling coastal town with plenty going on.
- **Tower Gardens Park, Skegness.** This large local park sits opposite the seafront and has good play areas.
- **Skegness Seafront.** Definitely worth strolling along at any time of year. There are fish and chip shops in abundance.

14

Frampton Marsh

The Wash Trail

What can you see?

Frampton Marsh hosts an excellent nature day. The staff at this new RSPB reserve offer lots of advice and information and have plenty of activities available for children to help them learn about marsh life during their walk. There is also an opportunity to watch boats heading down the Witham Mouth from Boston.

Kiddiwalks in Lincolnshire

14

Getting there *From the A16 in Kirton, south of Boston, turn right at the roundabout towards Frampton village. Follow this road all the way down for approximately three miles until you reach the end with a signpost marked 'Frampton Marsh' where you will find a car park.*

Length of walk 2¼ miles.
Time Allow 2 hours.

Terrain Flat, easy terrain in most sections. Some hill climbing up the sea bank. Can be very muddy in sections. Wellies recommended. Not suitable for pushchairs or bikes.
Dogs Dogs are not allowed in the nature reserve. They are allowed on some of the trails.
Start/Parking The RSPB free car park. Donations are welcome. (GR TF356392).
Map OS Explorer 249 Spalding & Holbeach.

The Walk

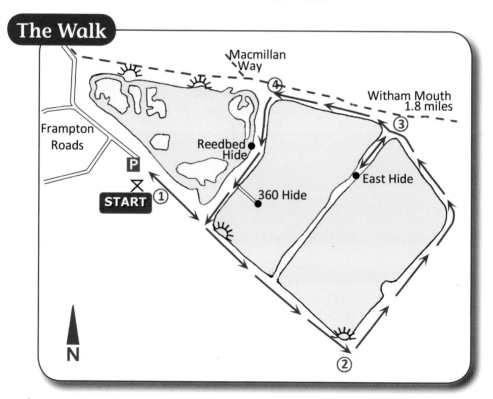

Tide Times Timetable available from the visitor centre.

Refreshments A tea/coffee machine and limited drinks and snacks are available at the visitor centre. Picnic tables and toilets are available on site. Plenty of benches on the trails.

1 Head straight to the visitor centre and turn left to follow the path with the marsh ponds on your left. You may see birdwatchers with their telescopes. Remind your children to be quiet when passing them. Continue past the bench and walk ahead where the path merges onto the road, bearing left. At the end of this section, the road merges into a path where it meets a wooden barrier. At the end of this path climb the set of wooden steps leading up to the sea bank and turn left. This section can be quite muddy after wet weather and it can be especially windy.

2 Continue along the sea bank through a wooden gate and follow the trail, which curves to the left at the end. From this point you can see boats and cargo vessels sailing down the bank from Boston into the Witham Mouth.

3 After following the trail to the left, continue along the sea bank until you reach a set of steps and a wooden gate marked 'Visitors Centre & Hide'. Turn left. There can be cows wandering around on the opposite bank, but they are fenced from your walk. If you want to visit the bird hide, follow

◆ Fun Things to See and Do ◆

Activity packs are available at the visitor centre for children to complete while on their trail. Bring your **binoculars**. If you don't have any, they can be hired. Spend time viewing wildlife and water birds in the hides. Have a look through the **large telescopes** in the visitor centre. The RSPB run children's **activity days** such as pond dipping. Check out their website for further details www. rspb.org.uk/framptonmarsh the marked path to the left, otherwise continue to the right. Carry on along the path. From this section you often see horses and there is a bench where you can rest.

❹ The path leads down to a fork, where you bear left (going right will add another 1½ miles to your walk, along the Reedbed Trail). Follow the path all the way back down past two more hides. At the end, go through a gate and turn right to the visitor centre and car park.

Cattle grazing alongside the Witham Mouth.

◆ Background Notes ◆

Frampton Marsh is situated on The Wash – one of Europe's best wetlands for wildlife. The major part of this RSPB reserve lies in the area known as the Scalp. The reserve supports breeds such as redshank, oystercatcher, reed bunting, meadow pipit and skylark. It is also a good place to watch hares, dragonflies, barn owls and flocks of geese.

Freiston Shore, a smaller nature reserve, lies 13 miles to the north. The tide comes in all the way to this reserve if you fancy walking closer to the sea. Check out the tide times. Timetables available from the visitor centre or telephone 01205 724678; www.rspb.org.uk/freistonshore

MAKING THE MOST OF YOUR DAY
- **Frampton village.** Beautiful traditional English village with a family pub, the Moores Arms.
- **Whaplode Maize Maze**, near Spalding to the south. For the summer holidays only, this maze grows 7ft high. It is lots of fun and there is plenty to keep children busy. www.mazeinmaize.co.uk

Culverthorpe Walks

The Great Farming Adventure

Harvest-time at Culverthorpe.

Culverthorpe Walks lies between Sleaford and Grantham around the country estate of the stunning Culverthorpe Hall. What is attractive about this walk is the amount of arable farming and livestock to be seen, including horses. There is also a large fishing lake. It offers the privilege of walking through the main gates and alongside the hall, its cottages and farm buildings. It is an easy route to follow in spite of the rather detailed directions!

Getting there *From the A15 south of Sleaford, turn off to Oasby and Culverthorpe. Or from the A52, east of Grantham, turn off towards Oasby, and follow the road east towards Culverthorpe. There is a brown sign for Culverthorpe Lakes on the road between Oasby and Culverthorpe.*

Length of walk 3¼ miles.
Time Allow 2½ hours.
Terrain Generally flat, with one large hill; could be muddy underfoot in some areas. Not suitable for pushchairs or bikes.
Dogs Signs state that dogs should be kept on leads. Livestock in some fields.
Start/Parking Free car park at the lakeside (GR TF019399).

The Walk

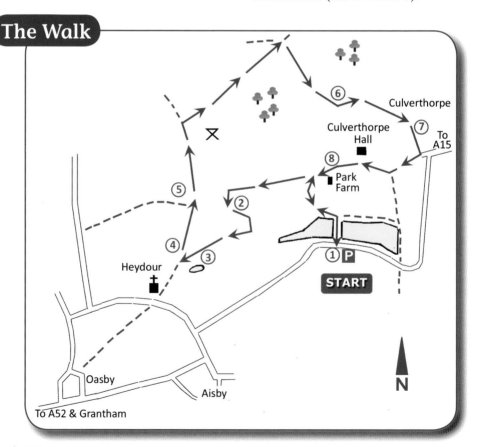

Culverthorpe

Culverthorpe Hall

To A15

Park Farm

Heydour

Oasby

Aisby

To A52 & Grantham

N

START

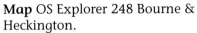

Map OS Explorer 248 Bourne & Heckington.

Refreshments None available on the route. There is one picnic table at the car park. No toilets. Nearest refreshments are at Welby, beyond Oasby.

1 From the car park entrance, turn left and follow a trail through to a gate leading to a road. Turn right onto the road and follow it as it gently rises and bends to the left where you will see a stone house to your right. Cross the stile before the house and continue until you meet a path which forks. Bear left and follow a graded track along this field edge.

2 At the end of the field, turn left by the post showing a waymarker and carry on down a grassy path. This path bends to the left and gives you the option to take a short-cut on your right, or to follow our route round to the left. The grassy track enters another field where you will see a 'Private' sign on a wooden post. Continue ahead by the waymarker. Continue to follow the hedge line on your right and round the corner until you see Heydour church spire on your left.

3 You approach a wooden stile which takes you into a field with a large nesting pond. Cross the field along the fence line and leave over the wooden stile at the end. You cross onto a track immediately ahead towards another stile on a small wooden bridge by the public footpath marker. Follow the grassy path round to another gate and wooden stile. Go through the gate and follow the grassy path ahead.

◆ Fun Things to See and Do ◆

There are many things to look out for on this farming walk. Make an 'I-Spy' sheet for the children which could include wasps' nest, horses, 'Beware of the Bull' sign, equestrian area for show-jumping, sheep, pheasant farm, Culverthorpe Hall, tractors, farming machinery, giant hay bales, Culverthorpe lake, fishermen. **Harvest** is an excellent time to do this walk if you want your children to see the farmers busy out in the fields.

4 On this path you will see a church in the distance. Turn right at the end towards another wooden stile. On the fence is a 'Beware of the Bull' sign; however, I have yet to come across a bull in this field. It is a small field, usually containing horses and sheep and it is easy to see which animals are grazing here. Cross this field with the hedge on your right, directly over to the wooden stile at the end. (If there is a bull in this field, back track your way round to the shortcut.)

5 Coming out of the field, walk across the tarmac track to a small bridge with a marker on it. Cross the bridge and follow the field round to the right. As you follow this path round you will notice the area on your left is used for equestrian activities. (The shortcut brings you out to this point.)

6 Cross a small bridge into the next field and continue ahead. Follow the edge of this field to the end until you come to a hedgerow where there is a marker post. Follow this short trail through the trees and bear right into the next field, then immediately left where you will see a 'Conservation Area' sign. This is an ideal **picnic spot**. Head towards the woods at the end of the field, with the hedge on your left. You cross a small wooden bridge into the next field by a waymarker post. Continue ahead.

7 At the end of this field you will see a 'Private – No public Right of Way' sign. Turn right and head up the field. At the top of the hill is another 'Private' sign. Continue ahead and bear right, before bearing left into the next field. Follow the edge of the field with the hedge on your left. The field bends but you continue on it until you come to the edge where there is a wooden post marked 'Absolutely no access'. Turn left here along the edge of the next field. As you continue ahead, you will have a glimpse of Culverthorpe Hall and its grounds. A bridge leads to a pheasant farm, you can cross this and take a peep through the fence at the pheasants.

8 At the end of this field you will see a wooden post marked 'Private' beside a wooden bridge, which you cross. You then have a short walk through a wooded area .This area can be quite muddy underfoot. Cross a second wooden bridge into a farming field and turn left. Follow the edge of the field until you reach the road. Turn right and follow the road to a T-junction with a sign marked 'Culverthorpe and No through Road'. Turn right and head towards the large metal gates which lead into the country estate. Go through and follow the road all the way past Culverthorpe Hall, the stable blocks and grazing animals. You feel very privileged to be walking through such finery! Leave the country estate at a cattle grid and gates. Turn left past a collection of farm buildings. Cross the wooden stile and continue back down the road towards the car park. There is an opportunity to view parts of the lake through an enclosed fenced path on your left, if you wish to extend your walk.

Inquisitive locals.

◆ Background Notes ◆

Culverthorpe Hall was built around 1679 for Sir John Newton. This was some six years before building commenced on Belton House, 8 miles away. It still stands as an eight-bedroom private residence today in 3,000 acres, including two large fishing lakes. There is a lot of conservation taking place around this area, with many arable fields, as well as livestock. It is also a popular area for equestrian activities. Culverthorpe Lakes are used for private fishing.

MAKING THE MOST OF YOUR DAY
- **Belton House** – a National Trust Property near Grantham. www.nationaltrust.org.uk
- **Cogglesford Mill**, to the east of Sleaford town centre. Free award-winning working watermill on the River Slea. www.cogglesfordmillsleaford.co.uk
- **Cranwell Aviation Heritage Centre**, 3 miles west of Sleaford on the A17. Free to discover the history of RAF Cranwell with flight simulator, interactive, video theatre, etc. www.heartoflincs.com

The Hills and Hollows

The Gingerbread Trail

Having fun along the way.

The Hills and Hollows is an area of footpaths over arable farmland and woodland on the south-east edge of Grantham. This beautiful hill-top follows part of the Gingerbread Way, a 25-mile circular route around the town which includes a section of Hall's Hill. The walk offers the eye seasonal changes throughout the year. From its fields of poppies in late spring, the abundance of cornfields and harvest in the summer to the brown leaves and berries in autumn and the snow-covered paths in winter. Once at the top of the ridge you are greeted with stunning views across the town. It makes a wonderful sunset walk.

The Hills and Hollows

 Getting there *The Hills and Hollows can be found from the A52 on the east side of Grantham. If you are coming from the east, drive past the army barracks on the A52 to Somerby Hill. At the bottom of the hill is a Shell garage. Immediately after the garage is Cold Harbour Lane, (there is a no through road sign marked 'unsuitable for HGV'. Turn right and follow the road up the hill until it becomes a single lane track. You can park at the top. Alternatively, if you are coming from the west, drive all the way out of Grantham on the A52. Pass McDonald's on your right and continue ahead until you see the Shell garage on your left on Somerby Hill. Immediately before this is a left turn into Cold Harbour Lane. Follow that road to the top.*

Length of walk 2½ miles.
Time Allow 2 hours.
Terrain Flat, easy terrain but not suitable for pushchairs.

Dogs Keep dogs under control.
Start/Parking Off-road parking at the top of the hill. (GR SK928352)

◆ Fun Things to See and Do ◆

There is a lot of wildlife to be seen on this walk. In particular you will come across **rabbits**. This is good way of explaining how rabbits live underground and survive. There are many warrens to be seen, particularly in the woods. If you do this walk at sunset, you will see dozens of them out feeding. Also in the woods, you will hear many different **bird songs**. See how many different types of song you can hear. **Guess the crops.** There are several different arable fields on this walk. Explain to the children what is growing in each field (easiest to play in spring and summer!) and what each crop will go on to make. **Where is it?** Play I-spy on top of the hill where the views are best. See if you can find the following town landmarks: St Wulfram's church, Grantham hospital, The Maltings, the white water tower, Belvoir Castle, Belton House and Belmont Tower. After snowfall, the hills which lead off this walk are popular for **sledging**.

The Walk

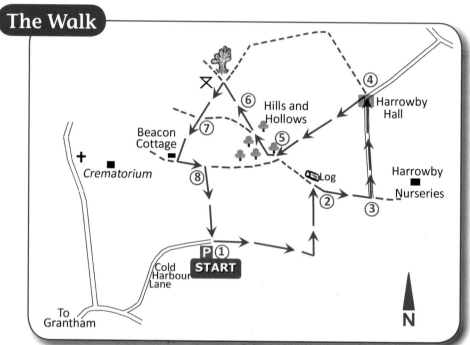

Map OS Explorer 247 Grantham, Bottesford & Colsterworth.
Refreshments None available on the walk but Grantham has many amenities. The nearby Fox & Hounds at Old Somerby also offers great family meals in a delightful setting.

1 At the top of the hill is a large green gate next to an enclosure of trees. Head through the trees and follow the path between two fields. (Alternatively, you can walk along the field edge on your right.) Follow this path for about 600 m until it bends to the left. Continue for another 300 m. You can catch glimpses of the fields beside you and sometimes you can watch the farmers at work.

2 At the end, the footpath forks beside a large fallen tree. Turn right. Follow this footpath which runs between two fields again until you reach the end.

3 Turn left onto the road which is a restricted byway. This is part of the Harrowby Hall estate. Follow the road to a collection of farm buildings and cottages at the end.

4 There is a large metal gate on your left. Go through and follow the track between two fields. Look out for sheep on your right. There are excellent views across the vales from here.

5 At the end, the track goes through the wooden gate. Walk towards the public footpath sign. Take the path to your right which leads into the woods and follow the main path. (This is a small area of woodland where it is easy to explore without getting lost.) Look out for rabbits. This area of woodland is known as the Hills and Hollows.

Poppies grow in abundance in late spring.

6 The main path leads out of the woods towards a large grassy bank. Continue ahead. (You will see another public footpath sign on your left and, in the summer, you may wish to walk along a path through this meadow instead, to cut across the field.) Otherwise, continue on the main track where you will see a large fallen tree on your right. Turn left at the end. From here you have wonderful views of St Wulfram's church and Grantham. You are now on an area known as Hall's Hill.

7 Follow the hedgeline and walk through a short enclosure of trees and back up a slope across to the next field. Continue ahead towards Beacon Cottage.

8 Follow the path round to the left by the public footpath signs. Don't forget to glance back as you walk along the track – the views are beautiful. This track leads you all the way back to the start.

Kiddiwalks in Lincolnshire

◆ Background Notes ◆

The area called **Hills and Hollows** was once a quarry from which the stone to build Harrowby Hall was extracted. The hillocks were created from farmers' waste becoming overgrown. In 1979, there was a local outcry when Lincolnshire County Council wanted to use the site for landfill, and in 2010 the site again became threatened and was up for sale as a possible dirt bike circuit. It was saved, however, when the local parish council bought it. At the time of publication, the Hills and Hollows is undergoing moderate changes, with tree planting and the possibility of fencing to protect the area and turn it into a nature reserve.

Hall's Hill is named after a family of wool merchants who lived at Hill Place (now Grantham House, owned by the National Trust).

Cold Harbour Lane was known locally as 'Monkey Millard's Lane' after the Rev Edwin Millard who kept a small zoo at his home at the top of the hill during the First World War.

The majestic 13th-century **St Wulfram's church**, which dominates views of the town, has the sixth highest spire in England at 282 ft. It is located in the old part of Grantham and also serves refreshments. www.stwulframs.org.uk

MAKING THE MOST OF YOUR DAY
- **Wyndham Park**, Manthorpe Road, Grantham. Lovely town park with the River Witham running through it. Play areas, river walks, tea rooms and a paddling pool. (From the bottom of Cold Harbour Lane, turn right and right again following the 'College and Crematorium' sign. Follow this road across the first crossroads, and turn left at the second. The car park is at the bottom of the road.)
- **Woolsthorpe Manor**, Colsterworth, south of Grantham on the A1. The 17th-century manor house where Sir Isaac Newton was born. There are lots of interactive experiments and activity days. www.nationaltrust.org.uk

Grantham Canal and Denton Reservoir

Swan Lake

Meeting the friendly locals.

The Grantham Canal was once derelict and over-grown, but thanks to years of hard work and dedication from its many supporters, it has been transformed to make way for an excellent cycle and walking route which links Grantham to Nottingham. This walk begins outside the picturesque village of Harlaxton and continues towards the equally beautiful Denton. Here you can see the reservoir and explore the countryside away from the canal towpath.

Kiddiwalks in Lincolnshire

17

Getting there *Take the A607 from Grantham to Harlaxton. Once in Harlaxton, turn right at the crossroads beside the Gregory Arms down a road call The Drift. This walk begins at the bottom of The Drift by the small bridge.*

Length of walk 2½ miles.
Time 2 hours.
Terrain Flat, easy terrain. Pushchair- and cycle-friendly only on the canal towpath.
Dogs Keep dogs under control as some fields have horses in them.
Start/Parking The Drift where there is roadside parking. (GR SK882338).

Map OS Explorer 247 Grantham, Bottesford & Colsterworth.
Refreshments The nearby stylish and family-friendly Gregory Arms in Harlaxton, where there is also a shop.

❶ At the bottom of The Drift, cross the small canal bridge. Immediately after crossing, turn right and go down to the towpath, then double back under the bridge marked no.66.

❷ Follow the towpath for 1¼ miles until you reach Denton Wharf Bridge (no.65). This part of the walk is where you will notice the swans and their cygnets. There are also lots of ducks who love to be fed and this is a

The Walk

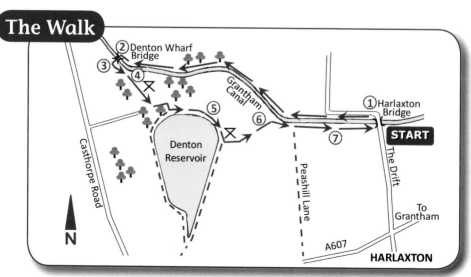

② Denton Wharf Bridge
③
④
Grantham Canal
⑤
⑥
① Harlaxton Bridge
START
⑦
Casthorpe Road
Denton Reservoir
The Drift
Peashill Lane
To Grantham
A607
HARLAXTON
N

Grantham Canal and Denton Reservoir

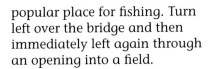

popular place for fishing. Turn left over the bridge and then immediately left again through an opening into a field.

3 Bearing left across the field, follow the hedge along a track until you come to an opening in the next hedge at the end of the field.

4 Cross the next meadow along the diagonal track to the far corner. This is my favourite **picnic spot**. Climb the stile at the end of the meadow and turn left down a wooded track, then immediately right across a narrow bridge. Head towards Denton Reservoir which is clearly signed. Bear left towards the embankment and bear left again at the top to see the reservoir.

5 To extend this walk by half a mile, you can circumnavigate the reservoir in an anti-clockwise direction. My walk, however, continues left towards a picnic table. It's worth taking a rest-stop here as this is quite pretty and there is always plenty of wildlife on the reservoir. From the picnic table, continue left and head towards a public footpath sign with steps leading down to a wooden footbridge over a feeder stream.

6 Continue along the right-hand edge of two fields. There are sometimes horses in the field on your left. Cross the second field, staying on the right-hand edge of the field along the hedge. At the end of this field you reach a track. Immediately

◆ Fun Things to See and Do ◆

Every spring, walkers meander down to the canal to see the **swans and their new babies** all gracefully gliding together. (Don't get too close as they may become aggressive whilst protecting their young.) Moorhens and ducks are also a common sight, so don't forget to bring some bread crumbs. Stroke the **horses** that often come over to the fence edge to greet walkers. There are many small streams leading off this walk, which can make it a lot of fun for **sailing home-made boats**. Boats can be made using old corks, driftwood, sticks, and leaves. Why not build the boats during your walk?

The towpath at Harlaxton.

Grantham Canal and Denton Reservoir

across the track is a hedge with a slight opening onto a public footpath. In summer it can get overgrown and is not always easy to see. Ask the children to rustle around to see who can find the 'secret entrance'. Cross the stile and a small wooden bridge.

7 Cross this field, bearing right until you reach the end and cross a stile into the next field. From here we leave the fields and bear left towards a tunnel of woodland which takes you alongside the canal. Follow the canal path back to the bridge where you started.

◆ Background Notes ◆

The **Grantham Canal** was part of a 33-mile navigation built in 1797 to transport coal from Nottingham to Grantham. The round trip for transporting coal, including loading and unloading, was ten days. On this walk you can see the winding hole, a wide part of the canal where boats could turn round. The role of Denton Reservoir was to feed water to the canal. In 1830, the use of the canal lessened as it competed with railways, and it finally closed in 1936. In the 1950s, canal bridges were often flattened to make way for roads, and like many of the canals it became overgrown and unsightly, attracting mass fly-tipping. In the 1970s, the Grantham Canal Restoration Society was formed and over time they brought life and beauty back to the canal for all to enjoy. They rely on volunteers and donations to continue their excellent work. www.granthamcanal.com

MAKING THE MOST OF YOUR DAY
- **Harlaxton.** Take a stroll through this award-winning traditional village. It has a pleasant children's play area with stunning countryside views at the south end of the village (signposts marked 'recreational area'). A 15-minute walk from The Drift.
- **Harlaxton Manor.** Famous for the filming of the 1999 Hollywood blockbuster *The Haunting* starring Liam Neeson and Catherine Zeta-Jones. This 19th-century manor is closed to the public (it is now the UK campus of Evansville University, USA), but can be viewed from the gates. www.ueharlax.ac.uk/harlaxton

18

Bellmount Tower and Londonthorpe Woods

Rapunzel's Tower

On the edge of the woods.

Bellmount Tower sits high on a hill overlooking the majestic Belton House and with breathtaking views of the south Lincolnshire countryside. The walk begins at Londonthorpe Wood, a new wood, and leads up the hill to ancient woodland and through a shadowy tree-lined avenue to Bellmount Tower, and finally takes you through lovely meadows. This makes a particularly enchanting summer evening walk.

Bellmount Tower and Londonthorpe Woods

Getting there *From the A607, just north of Grantham, take the turn towards Belton House (well signposted). Follow the road through Belton village, turning right at the sign for Barkston Heath. Follow this road until you come to a junction shortly after a cottage. Turn right and follow the road for about 1½ miles. Just before the T-junction at the end, you will see a Woodland Trust car park on your right, for Londonthorpe Wood.*

Length of walk 3 miles.

Time 2 hours.

Terrain Hilly. It can be muddy underfoot after wet weather, particularly at the top of the hill. Not suitable for pushchairs or bikes.

Dogs Keep dogs on a lead around livestock.

Start/Parking Londonthorpe Wood free car park (GR SK945379).

Map OS Explorer 247 Grantham, Bottesford & Colsterworth

Refreshments The nearest facilities are at Belton Garden Centre, or you could take a picnic.

The Walk

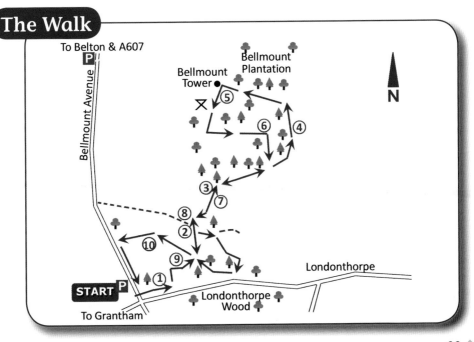

Kiddiwalks in Lincolnshire

1 Leaving the car park, turn right and cross the road. Immediately on your left is a wooden gate marked 'Londonthorpe Wood'. Go through the gate and continue towards a cluster of trees. Follow this path as it glides by the edge of the wood and curves to the left towards woodland. Follow the track through the woodland.

2 At the end of the woodland track, turn right and follow the path towards a wooden bench. Continue until the path divides into two. Bear left and follow the path towards the hedge. At the T-junction, bear left again towards a wooden gate and stile. *Dog owners – be aware that sheep are often grazing in these fields.*

3 Cross the stile and turn immediately right to follow the edge of the field towards the next stile. Cross the second stile and walk diagonally across the field towards the wooden gate at the end. Crossing the third stile, you enter the woods that lead to Bellmount Tower. Follow the track through the woods. This section of the walk is quite hilly and often muddy underfoot during wet weather.

4 At the end of this trail, follow the path along the bottom of the wood, where the hedge is to your right along a broad swathe of grass. You will be walking along a narrow path which winds around the trees as you gradually climb through the woods. Continue

◆ Fun Things to See and Do ◆

During snowy times in **winter**, Bellmount Tower is popular for sledging. In spring, there is an abundance of lambs and baby deer to be seen. In **summer**, the meadow in Londonthorpe Wood is a joy to run through, and in **autumn** there is the fascination of watching the trees change colour and shed their leaves. The dense wood at the top of the hill is popular with **deer**. If you are very quiet, you may see them. Making **elf and fairy houses** – bring string and scissors with you. Using small twigs help the children make tiny ladders and doorways in the tree stumps and tiny elf gardens with stones, leaves and cones.

Bellmount Tower and Londonthorpe Woods

along this footpath to a large opening and grassy avenue. Turn left, to see the majestic Bellmount Tower in the distance. Walk towards the tower and through the gate at the end. This is my favourite **picnic spot**. The views are beautiful here and you can see Belton House directly ahead.

5 From the tower, turn left and head across the top of the field towards a wooden gate. Pass through the gate and follow the path. Where the path splits in two, bear left. Follow this path as it bends to the left, leading to a large grassy clearing. Continue until you see a main turning on your right.

6 Turn down this grassy slope and follow it to the bottom of the hill. At the bottom of the hill, turn right through the trees and follow the same track back towards the wooden gate and stile you previously came through.

7 Crossing the stile, again walk diagonally across the field towards a second stile. On crossing this, remain along the hedge line as you reach a third stile on your left and cross it back into Londonthorpe Wood.

8 Take the path ahead, then

The impressive Bellmount Tower.

bear left and left again where the paths meet. This will lead towards an enclosure of trees and bushes. Stay ahead until you see the end of the wood where the path forks and take the right path into the trees, remaining on this path as it curves around the edge of the woods.

9 You will meet a section where the path breaks into three routes. Take the middle path which wanders through the meadow and offers good views. At the end of this path, bear left and head right at the next junction through the woods. Once out of the

wooded area follow the path past the meadow and continue.

10 The path will again divide – carry on ahead and follow the track back down towards the road, passing a wooden fence. You are now at the edge of Londonthorpe Wood where you will see a gate. Do not go through this gate, instead turn left and follow the hedge line for 200 m until you reach a second gate. This is the gate you came in through at the start and takes you back to the car park.

◆ Background Notes ◆

Bellmount Tower is owned by the National Trust and opens its doors only in September. It was built around 1750 by the Brownlow family who lived in Belton House. Indeed, from the tower you can look down and see Belton House immediately ahead. The tower is rumoured to have had many uses – for aristocratic picnics, as an observatory and as a private library. Other views are that the tower was simply a folly, a feature to be seen from the house.

Londonthorpe Wood has been owned by the Woodland Trust since 1991. It has gradually been developed from agricultural land into a wonderful wood and meadow with paths leading through its 155 acres. www.woodlandtrust.org.uk

MAKING THE MOST OF YOUR DAY
- **Belton House**, Grantham, has a large adventure playground, formal gardens, extensive grounds and plenty of picnic areas. www.nationaltrust.org.uk
- **Belton Garden Centre**, opposite Belton House, is a lovely garden centre in a tranquil setting with children's play area, animals to visit and a coffee shop. www.beltongardencentre.co.uk
- **Syston Fruit Farm.** Signposted on the A607 before Barkston, just to the north of Belton. This farm is a joy for children to go fruit picking in season. It sits on top of a hill with a farm shop, café and play area.

Bourne Woods

The Nightingale Trail

The Ponds are a good place to rest awhile.

Bourne Woods is a beautiful recreational woodland. It is easy to find, has ample parking and well laid out routes, picnic areas and a children's play area. The Nightingale Trail through the wood is a pretty and varied route suitable for the adventurous.

Kiddiwalks in Lincolnshire

Getting there *The wood lies 2 miles west of Bourne on the A151 Bourne to Grantham road. It is well signposted as you approach it.*

Length of walk 3 miles.
Time 2 hours.
Terrain Pushchair- and cycle-friendly only on the main circular route around the woods, not on the Nightingale Trail.
Dogs Keep dogs under control.
Start/Parking The free car park at the wood. (GR TF079204).
Map OS Explorer 248 Bourne & Heckington.
Refreshments The nearest facilities are in Bourne, 2 miles away but there are plenty of picnic tables in the wood.

❶ From the rear of the car park, walk into the woods by the posts with the sign marked 'This car park closes at 7 pm'. At the main path, turn left and walk towards the main noticeboard at the crossroads by the bench.

❷ Facing the noticeboard, take the path to the right which leads into the woods. You will notice posts with orange markers on them throughout this walk and this helps you know you are on the right path. Follow this path through the woods until the path forks; bear left and continue. You will see a picnic bench on your right. Where the path joins another trail, turn left, where you will see an orange marker post and continue ahead. This section could be muddy underfoot after rain. At a T-junction, turn right by the orange-marker post and follow the trail heading east. This section is quite good for den building. At the T-junction turn left onto the main path.

❸ By the public footpath sign beside the stone bridge, divert off the path into the woods and do a semi-circular loop through the woodland. There are many bird boxes and animal activity in this section. You leave the loop through a mass of fern and go back onto the main path. You will have gone up about 300 m in total. This inside section is also quite good for den building.

❹ As you continue along this long section of path, you will see a small circular maze on your left. It improves with growth towards the end of summer. After the maze and further up the path, you will notice a third area to your

The Walk

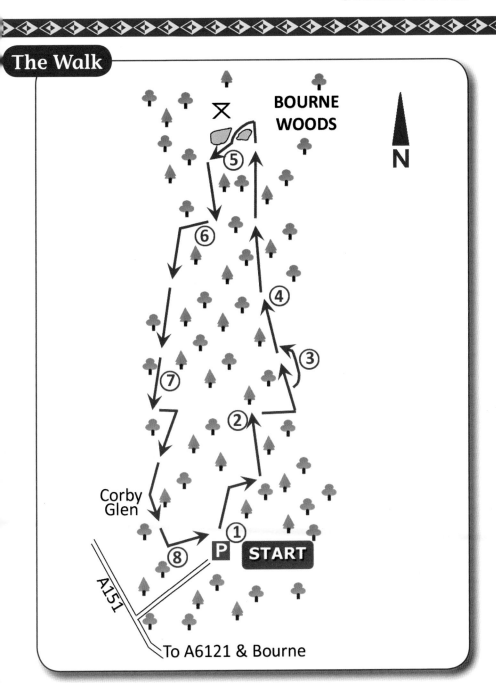

BOURNE
WOODS

N

⑤

⑥

④

③

⑦

②

①

Corby
Glen

⑧

P

START

A151

To A6121 & Bourne

left which is also good for den building. You pass a major junction on your left as the path starts to rise gently, and the deciduous wood begins to give way to pine wood on your left.

5 Turn left at the sign for 'The Ponds'. Follow the path, bearing left to the first pond. Continue to a bench which is my favourite **picnic spot**. This is a beautiful place in summer though it can be very muddy underfoot after continuous wet weather. From the bench you can walk to the right to see a second large pond. To carry on, from the bench head left into the woods (you will see a second seat on your right) and follow the path at a steady climb through the trees which leads you back onto the main path. Turn left.

6 Continue down the path. You will see a main cycle path on your left by a signpost. Go past a wooden bench where almost immediately there is a grassy semi-circular bank on your right. There is a small track leading into the woods at this point which isn't marked. Follow this path through the woods, where you will see an orange-marker post further up and three carved wooden mushrooms.

◆ Fun Things to See and Do ◆

The beauty of this trail is that it takes you into a quiet and little-used area of the wood. You can sometimes **spot deer running** through the woods and crossing the track in front of you. At the Ponds you might see kingfishers and herons. **Den building** can be great fun. In the summer, the Friends of Bourne Wood hold a Family Den Building Day. To make a great tree den, position it close to other trees for support. Once you get the frame right, the rest comes easily. Try using the guide on the 'How to make a Survival Shelter' activity sheet on www.wildlifewatch.org.uk if you need some help.

7 You now follow a small woodland trail and where the path meets a small T-junction, turn left. At the first crossroads, continue ahead. At the second crossroads is a bench, continue ahead. The path begins to climb to a third crossroads. Turn left. Further down this path is a small clearing in the trees by an orange marker post, turn right and follow the path.

8 At the next main crossroads, turn left by the orange marker post. This path returns you to the crossroads by the noticeboard. From here, take the fourth path which leads you back to the car park and play area.

Building a den.

Kiddiwalks in Lincolnshire

◆ Background Notes ◆

Bourne Woods is a quiet, ancient woodland which has belonged to the Forestry Commission since 1926. The area is managed for conservation, recreation and timber production. The wood is believed to have been here since the 11th century. Deep in the woods are two lakes called the Ponds, which were dug in 1972 to act as a watering hole for the local wildlife. If you visit at dawn or dusk, you can often see deer drinking from them. Other animals seen around the area are foxes, grey squirrels, owls, snakes and bats.

MAKING THE MOST OF YOUR DAY

- **Bourne Outdoor Pool.** Ideal on a hot day. There is a main heated pool, a toddler pool and plenty of space to lounge around. www. bourneoutdoorswimmingpool.org
- **Grimsthorpe Castle.** This lies between Grantham and Bourne and is perfect for picnics and bike riding. Lovely gardens for children to explore and a good adventure playground in the woods. www. grimsthorpe.co.uk
- **Hansen's Chocolate House**, Folkingham. If you really want to reward (or bribe) your children, try this wonderful chocolate shop bursting with the history of chocolate and, of course, lots of wonderful hand-made chocolate in this lovely village. www. mrchocolate.co.uk
- **Corby Glen.** If you're heading north-west on the A151, why not visit this quaint stone village with its pretty market square and historic buildings? It has a village shop, a pub and a pleasant play area for the children.

20

Deeping Lakes

The Secret Lake

Looking for swans on the lake.

What makes Deeping Lakes so fascinating is that few people seem to know about it. To those who don't live in the southeast part of Lincolnshire, it remains secret and hidden away, making it more special when you do stumble across it, and meaning that it is usually very quiet there.

Getting there *Follow the B1166 out of Deeping St James towards Crowland. Turn left to go over the railway at the level crossing. Follow this road until you reach a sharp left bend. On the bend you will see a sign for Deeping Lakes to the right. Follow the sign down the track to the free car park.*

Length of walk 1½ miles.
Time Allow 1½ hours.
Terrain Flat, easy terrain. Not suitable for pushchairs or bikes.
Dogs Keep dogs under control around livestock and wildlife.

Start/Parking The nature reserve car park where there is free parking. (GR TF185080).
Map OS Explorer 235 Wisbech & Peterborough North.
Refreshments The nearest refreshments are in Deeping St James so why not take a picnic?

❶ Leaving the car park, turn right onto the road. You will see a sign marked 'Visitors' Trail'. Follow the road to the end until you see a series of gates. Turn right and follow the fenced path to a bird hide. From there follow the trail to your right. You will approach a bench on your right

The Walk

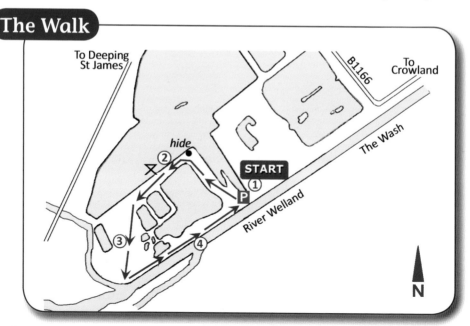

by a lake which makes a pleasant place to stop.

❷ As you follow the path, you will have glimpses of the lake on your right. At the end follow the arrows pointing left. There are excellent views of the lake on the right along this section, with swans in abundance. There is a bench here at my favourite **picnic spot**.

❸ Continue to follow the signs directing you left, along the path among the trees and hedgerows. At the end you come to a metal gate and information board. Go through the gate and climb approximately 10 m uphill, then turn left. This final section of walk takes you along the banks of the River Welland.

Admiring a dragonfly.

❹ On this final stretch, cows may be grazing beside the river. Some may be on your pathway so if, like me, you

◆ Fun Things to See and Do ◆

Go on a **bone hunt**. There are many old bones lying around from various animals and birds. See if the children can find any, and guess which animal they came from, and from which part of the body. In summer you will find hundreds of stunning bright blue **dragonflies** along the trail. Sometimes if you hold out your hand, they will sit on it. Dance along with the dragonflies.

are not keen on approaching cattle, you can walk along the left of the bank to avoid them. However, I found them quite placid and obviously used to humans walking alongside them. My advice is to stay quiet and calm, and they shouldn't be a problem. At the end of this stretch is a large metal gate. Go through it and bear left along the bank to the next gate. Once through, turn right, back to the car park. Should you wish to extend your walk, try exploring the other lakes where there is an abundance of wildlife, ducks, geese and swans.

◆ Background Notes ◆

Deeping Lakes are owned by Lincolnshire Wildlife Trust. The area consists of a number of flooded gravel pits. The main lake was excavated in the late 1800s, whereas the two smaller lakes were excavated in the 1990s. The lake is known for its wildfowl and water bird communities, and over the years has been developed into a beautiful nature reserve thanks to volunteers who clock up as many as 5,000 hours of work a year. www.lincstrust.org.uk

Making the Most of Your Day
- **Burghley House**, Stamford. You can park, picnic and play in the vast grounds of this stately home for free. On a hot day, there is nothing better than going in the Garden of Surprises which has a series of water shoots, mazes and water showers. www.burghley.co.uk
- **Stamford** is a beautiful historic stone town well worth exploring. A river runs through the town and there are plenty of areas to relax or dine. Stamford is about 6 miles west of Deeping St James on the A16.
- **Uffington and Deeping St James** are both attractive villages. It is easy to find a country pub with a play area in either of these places. Uffington is just east of Stamford on the A16.